JOHN QUINCY ADAMS

JOHN QUINCY
ADAMS

FRED G. CLARKE

COLLIER BOOKS, NEW YORK

COLLIER-MACMILLAN, LIMITED, LONDON

Contents

JOHN QUINCY ADAMS

1

A Child of the American Revolution

BRAINTREE, MASSACHUSETTS, birthplace of two American Presidents, was in the eighteenth century a typical New England village. Its population consisted mostly of hard-working farmers. They were a sturdy and pious people whose lives of unremitting toil lacked luxury and were varied by only the simplest of pleasures. The men labored in the fields from sunup to sundown while the women at home wove the old-fashioned homespun cloth that protected the family during the cold northern winters. The products of the farm were bartered for groceries, dry goods and other necessities that could be obtained at Boston. With few means of public transportation, the trip to Boston, only nine miles away, was long and difficult. Those living on the seacoast went by water; those living farther inland made the journey over crude country roads in one-horse chaises, on horseback, or, if lower down in the social scale, on foot with panniers filled with merchandise slung on their shoulders.

Houses in town were mostly of brick, but wooden structures were more common in town and country. Except for the living room and the kitchen, they were generally unheated, and in the depth of winter a warming pad was used to take the chill off the bedclothing. Food was wholesome, if lacking in variety. Clothes were homemade, and plain, although girls often wore little ruffled aprons. Toys were rare, and candy was generally maple sugar or, on special occasions, rock candy from China. On the slab benches of the schoolhouses, children were taught spelling and reading from the Bible; the only reading book available was a text called *The New England Primer*. Blackboards were unknown, and few children owned their own books. They wrote with quill pens or with pencils made by melting lead into wooden molds. Few families owned books other than the Bible.

Such was the narrow, provincial, and almost unchanging world into which John Quincy Adams was born on July 11, 1767. But for the mutations of heredity and for the quickening pace of history, he might have been another New England farmer or townsman, loved by his family, respected by his neighbors, but whose footprints in the sands of time would not have survived his span of life. The first American ancestor of John Quincy was an English immigrant, Henry Adams, who came to Massachusetts from Somersetshire in 1636 and established a farm on a land grant he had received at Mount Wollaston, later known as Braintree. For four generations the Adamses remained men of humble condition and modest fortune, rising no higher in the social scale than village pastor. Then from the fifth generation came John Adams, leader in the American Revolution, diplomat, second President of the United States. His wife, Abigail Smith Adams, came from a long line of Protestant ministers in a time when ministers were the elite of New England society. One of the most cultured and well-educated women of her time, hers was a character of great nobility, extraordinary courage and high moral purpose. This was the family into which John Quincy Adams was born in 1767.

John Quincy was a child of the American Revolution. In the year of his birth, the British parliament passed the unpopular Townshend Acts, which levied duties on various products imported into the American colonies. The people of

Boston retaliated by organizing a boycott of certain products and purchasing substitutes of colonial manufacture. Their lead was soon followed throughout New England, and then in the middle and southern colonies. Three years later, five Boston citizens were killed in a riot at the Custom House. It was the bloodiest of a long series of clashes and became known as the Boston Massacre.

Soon afterwards, John Adams, now a prosperous Boston attorney, was elected Boston representative to the General Court. In the gathering conflict that threatened the country, he foresaw his new office as one which might well bring ruin upon himself and his family, and that night he confided his apprehensions to his wife. Abigail, then an expectant mother, burst into tears, but she stiffened the resolve of her husband with these words: "I am willing in this cause to run all risks with you and be ruined with you if you are ruined." Neither Adams nor his country were ruined. Just the contrary. But the disposition to behave courageously while expecting the worst was a distinguishing Adams trait that father would pass on to son.

Three years later, when John Quincy had passed his sixth birthday, the famous Boston Tea Party took place. Lord North thundered in parliament: "Boston has ever been the ringleader in all riots"—and Boston would be punished as an example to the other rebellious colonies. A series of coercive measures was enacted, the most severe being the closing of the port of Boston. Four regiments under General Gage were dispatched to Massachusetts to enforce the decrees. For Boston, a commercial center depending primarily on its seaborne trade, fishing and shipbuilding, the decree was virtually a death sentence. But the other colonies quickly rallied to the aid of the beleaguered city, and generous contributions in foodstuffs and money saved it from starvation. Encouraged in their defiance, the people of Boston struck back at their persecutors by making life unbearable for the occupation troops. On June 17, 1774, a convention of Massachusetts delegates elected John Adams, Samuel Adams, James Bowdoin and Thomas Cushing as their representatives to the first Continental Congress. Three weeks later, the delegation left for Philadelphia, the seat of the Congress.

A new and dangerous life began for the Adams family. For the next four years, except for a few brief visits, John Adams was away in Philadelphia, helping to organize a colony-wide resistance to the British. His wife and their four children moved from Boston to the relative safety of the Adams farm at Braintree. There, in the absence of her husband, Abigail Adams managed the home and farm, and cared for the children. Since the local school had closed when its one teacher left to join the Continental Army, young John's education began at home under the guidance of his mother and, later, Mr. Thaxter, his father's law clerk. Despite the informal atmosphere, Johnny was under a strict and exacting discipline. When he wanted to play truant to wander in the woods and hills, he was offered the choice of farming as a substitute for his lessons. After a day of ditching he was usually back with his books. By the age of ten he had read much of Shakespeare and Pope, and his mother had him read aloud to her a page or two each day from Rollin's *History of Antiquity*. Like most boys of that time, Johnny learned to ride at an early age. Before he was ten he was fetching the mail and news on horseback from Boston, some nine miles away—"the little post rider," his mother called him. Both parents had high hopes for their eldest son. From his earliest years, they trained him in the strict Puritan manner for a place of high eminence in the world.

Soon after John Adams's departure for Philadelphia, the omens of war began to multiply. General Gage prepared for hostilities, mounting cannon, digging entrenchments, throwing up breastworks, placing his regiments in strategic positions. His most fateful order was a command to seize the military caches of the colonists. The word was quickly passed to find new hiding places for the weapons and powder. On a

Sunday evening, Abigail and Johnny watched a silent procession of two hundred men returning from such an expedition. As the men passed her house, one of them called out to her and asked in jest if she wanted any powder. "No," she replied. "It is in good hands."

Such incidents became more numerous as Gage continued his search, until finally they climaxed in "the shot heard round the world," the battle of Lexington and Concord. The war was now a fact. Thousands of New Englanders moved in to surround Boston. The Adams house, where Abigail and her friends melted pewter spoons into bullets, was the scene of great excitement. In May, a rumor that the British had landed in Braintree created a panic. In the exodus, hundreds of men, women and children came flocking past the house. To these were added refugees from Boston begging for lodging and soldiers asking a drink, a meal, a place to bunk. No one was turned away. The war in its stark reality had come straight into Johnny's bedroom.

A month later, at three o'clock on a Saturday morning, June 17 ,1775, the Adams family was awakened by the thunder of cannon. The Battle of Bunker Hill had begun. Later in the day, Johnny, his hand firmly clasped by his mother's, walked with her to nearby Penn's Hill to watch the battle. In the distance they could see the clouds of smoke over burning Charleston. Mrs. Adams wrote her husband: "The day—perhaps the decisive—is come, on which the fate of America depends. . . . The battle . . . has not ceased yet, and it is now three o'clock Sabbath afternoon. . . . How many have fallen we know not. The constant roar of the cannon is so distressing that we cannot eat, drink or sleep." Among the fallen that day was Dr. Warren, a leading patriot and a friend of the family. Johnny remembered him well, for the doctor had saved his fractured finger from amputation.

The letters which came periodically from John Adams in Philadelphia described the politics, the conflicts, the decisions and the men of the Continental Congress. The one Johnny

would remember most clearly was written on July 3, 1776.
Abigail read it aloud to her children. "Yesterday," it began,
"the greatest question was decided which was ever debated in
America. . . . A Resolution was passed without one dissenting
colony 'that these United Colonies are, and of right ought to
be, free and independent states. . . .' " Mrs. Adams took young
John to Boston, where thousands of persons had gathered to
hear the Declaration read. "The bells rang, the privateers
fired," she wrote her husband, "the cannons were discharged. . . . After dinner the King's arms were taken down
from the State House and every vestige of him from every
place in which it appeared, and burnt in King Street. Thus
ends the royal authority in this state. And all the people shall
say Amen."

A few months earlier, the British, lacking the forces to
conquer Boston, had abandoned the town. From Penn's Hill
the Adams family had watched the departing ships, so numerous they looked like "a forest." Massachusetts was no longer
a theater of war. Only once again—a year later, when British
ships were sighted off Cape Ann—did fear of an impending
invasion seize the people. Like the other townsmen, the
Adams family prepared to evacuate. Fortunately the threat
proved to be a false alarm and they were not forced to leave.

In the winter of 1777 John Adams was at last reunited with
his family. After four years of distinguished service for the
Continental Congress, he had resigned his position to re-
establish his law practice. But the reunion was of short
duration. Congress summoned John Adams to proceed to
Paris and replace Silas Deane as a member of the American
mission to France. In view of the perils of sea travel in war-
time, it was decided that Mrs. Adams and the children, with
the exception of John Quincy, would remain at home. At that
time, in colonial America, the opportunity for education was
limited. Both John and Abigail Adams wanted their eldest
son to have the advantages a European education offered, and
so, at the age of ten, John Quincy Adams accompanied his

From Penn's Hill, Abigail Adams and young John Quincy watched the Battle of Bunker Hill.

John Quincy Adams was among the thousands who gathered in Boston to hear the Declaration of Independence read and to see the king's coat of arms burned.

father to France. Thus began two famous careers in American diplomacy.

On the 17th of February the Adamses sailed out of Marblehead harbor on board the frigate *Boston,* a sailing vessel overloaded with unmanageable cannon and manned by inexperienced sailors. The voyage lasted six weeks and, in Mr. Adams's words, was filled with "dangers, distresses, and hairbreadth escapes." On the first morning out, with most of the crew, and Johnny as well, seasick from the pitching and rolling of the ship, the *Boston* was chased for an entire day by an enemy man-of-war. By nightfall they had lost their pursuer, only to be overtaken in the Gulf Stream by a violent storm which lasted for three days, during which time it was almost impossible to stand upright. Ships stores and furnishings were smashed to bits, and the mainmast and a sailor were struck by lightning. When the seas had calmed, the *Boston* spied a sail and gave chase. The *Martha,* a British letter of marque, fired a shot that passed directly over the head of Mr. Adams, who was standing on the quarterdeck musket in hand. A broadside from the *Boston* forced the surrender of the *Martha.*

John Adams was proud of his son's courage, although in moments of great danger he often regretted he had brought the boy along. "Mr. Johnny's behavior," he wrote in his diary, "gave me a satisfaction that I cannot express; fully sensible of our danger, he was constantly endeavoring to bear it with manly patience, very attentive to me, and his thoughts constantly running in a serious strain." During the voyage young John learned the names and purpose of the sails. The captain instructed him in the mariner's compass and three of the French passengers aboard gave him lessons in French. On the 29th of March, the *Boston* put into the port of Bordeaux.

When they were settled in Paris, John Adams sent his son to a private boarding school at Passy, a small town on the outskirts of the city. Among his schoolmates were two grandsons of Benjamin Franklin, Silas Deane's son Jesse, and Charles Cochran of South Carolina. Maître Le Coeur taught the boys French and Latin as well as dancing, music and drawing. Johnny was a good pupil, attentive to his books, and made rapid progress in French. He visited the palace of Versailles and marveled at the splendor of its gardens and fountains. In Paris he walked the narrow, crooked streets and along the banks of the Seine; he saw the École Militaire, the leering gargoyles on the Cathedral of Notre Dame; he climbed to the top of the heights of Montmartre and of Menilmontant. These were, as he wrote his mother, among the "scenes of Magnificence" he had seen in the "city of lights." On Sundays, he went to the Bois de Boulogne, near his school in Passy, where he watched a company of children play simple French classics in the Théâtre des Petits Comédiens. It was here that his love for the theater began, and here also, as he confided to his wife many years later, that he lost his heart to one of the little actresses.

In Paris he made his first entries in a diary which his father had urged him to keep. He modestly wrote his mother: "I shall have the mortification a few years hence to read a great deal of my Childish nonsense, yet I shall have the Pleasure and the advantage of Remarking the several steps by which I advanced in taste, judgment and knowledge. A journal Book & a letter Book of a Lad of Eleven years Can not be expected to contain much of Science, Litterature, arts, wisdom or wit, yet it may serve to perpetuate many observations I make. . . ." This was the beginning of the diary that would one day be published in twelve large volumes by his son Charles Francis Adams and become one of the most famous of the memoirs written by American statesmen.

John Adams's assignment in Paris was brief. The treaty of alliance with France had been signed before he arrived. Since Benjamin Franklin had been appointed ambassador to the Court of Versailles, there was no further purpose to his remaining. On August 2, 1779, father and son were back in Boston. But hardly had Adams got his land legs back when Congress, advised of Spanish initatives for a general peace conference, ordered him back to Europe.

This time John Quincy preferred to remain at home to enter Andover Academy in preparation for Harvard. But his mother, with great ambitions for her son, persuaded him to go along with his younger brother Charles. She wrote John Quincy after his departure: "These are times in which a genius would wish to live. It is not in the still calm of life or the repose of a pacific station that great characters are formed. . . . Great necessities call out great virtues. . . . When a mind is raised and animated by scenes that engage the heart, then those qualities, which would otherwise lie dormant, wake into life and form the character of the hero and the statesman."

On December 18, 1779, Adams and his two boys landed in Spain after another venturesome voyage aboard the French frigate *Sensible*. From there they proceeded overland to Paris, where the boys were enrolled in the same boarding school at Passy that John Quincy had attended two years before. There they studied Greek and Latin and read selections from English historians and essayists. Early in 1781 John Adams left Paris on a mission to Holland. His sons accompanied him and while there attended the Amsterdam Latin School before transferring to the University of Leyden. From Leyden Johnny wrote his father that he and Charles were attending hour-long lectures on medicine each day and that he was studying Homer, Greek grammar and the Greek New Testament. But possibly the real point of the letter was a request for a few guilders to purchase a pair of ice skates so he could join the happy crowds skating on the frozen Dutch canals. A cheaper pair was also on sale, he hastened to add.

In the following year, John Quincy and Charles parted company. Homesick, Charles was sent back to Massachusetts, while his brother accompanied Francis Dana, an old friend of John Adams's, on a mission to Russia. Congress hoped that the United States might enter the Armed Neutrality pact formed by Catherine the Great and thus secure Russia's recognition of the republic. The diplomatic language at the Czarina's court was French, and Dana needed an interpreter and translator. At Adams's suggestion he consented to have Johnny, age fourteen, serve as his secretary. Dana and young Adams left Amsterdam on July 7, 1781, for St. Petersburg.

Dana's mission was unsuccessful. Catherine, as ruler of a monarchy, had little inclination to recognize a republic or to get more deeply embroiled with Great Britain, and she studiously ignored Dana. Having few official duties John Quincy concentrated on his books. There were no schools in the Russian capital because the nobles, who alone could afford to educate their children sent their sons to schools abroad, and the price of a tutor was beyond John Adams's pocketbook. John Quincy read Voltaire and Hume and Macauley, and he learned German, one of the first Americans of his time to do so.

Although he may never have seen the empress except from his hotel window, young Adams had formed opinions about autocratic Russia that were remarkably perceptive for a boy of fifteen. He wrote to his mother: "The government of Russia is entirely despotical; the sovereign is absolute in all the extent of the word. The persons, the estates, the fortunes of the nobility depend entirely upon his caprice. And the nobility has the same power over the people, the sovereign has over them. The nation is composed wholly of nobles and serfs, or, in other words, masters and slaves. . . . This form of government is disadvantageous to the sovereign, to the nobles and to the people. For, first it exposes the sovereign in every moment to revolution, of which there have been already four in the course of this century. . . ."

In October 1782, John Quincy left St. Petersburg for The Hague, little dreaming that a quarter of a century later he would return there as ambassador plenipotentiary. John Adams had been appointed a member with Franklin and Jay of the commission to draft the peace treaty with England. He made John Quincy his private secretary and took him to Paris, where Abigail and the other children would soon join them.

The boy had learned the rudiments of diplomacy in Rus-

sia, but in the next two years he would receive his full
initiation into all its mysteries. He was on speaking terms
with the members of the diplomatic corps, American, French
and British, and he soon knew the protocol of this world
as if he had been born into it. He developed a warm attachment for Thomas Jefferson when the latter replaced Franklin
as ambassador to France. The two would spend long evenings
together talking about science, politics, history and men.

On a visit to England young Adams sat in the visitors'
gallery of the House of Commons and marveled at the great
orators of the English parliament. It was the still bright
memory of the speeches of men like William Pitt, Charles
Fox, Sheridan and Lord North that inspired the rhetoric of
John Quincy Adams, the Congressman, in his later years.
Mostly he learned from his father, listening to the battles with
the British, the disagreements with the French, the quarrels
with Franklin. In the process, young Adams acquired most of
the qualities, the strong sides and the weak, of his father—
his brilliance, courage and integrity, as well as his inflex-
ibility and his obtuseness about human nature.

In February 1785, John Adams was appointed minister to
England, and as the family prepared to leave Paris, he invited his eldest son to accompany him as his private secretary. But John Quincy was of another mind. Although these
years in Paris had been the happiest in his life, and the appointment to the London embassy was hardly a trifle, he was
determined to return to the United States and resume his
studies at Harvard preparatory to the practice of law. As a
public servant his father's income had been seriously cur-
tailed, and young John was firmly resolved that "I will depend upon no one." "At least in America," he exclaimed in
his diary, "I can live *independent* and *free*; and rather than
live otherwise I should wish to die before the time when I
shall be left at my own discretion."

2

From Harvard Student
to Boston Lawyer

YOUNG ADAMS was far better equipped than most young men of his age for entrance into Harvard. He was fluent in French, German, Latin and Dutch; he was well versed in English and French literature; and from his father he had acquired a working knowledge of geometry, trigonometry and even some differential calculus. Nevertheless, he entered a preparatory school at Haverhill, and in the latter part of 1785, he was admitted to Harvard as a junior and granted free tuition as a token of appreciation for his father's services to his country.

There were one hundred and forty undergraduates at Harvard when John Quincy entered. Somewhat less forbidding than in Puritan times, the university was still an austere place governed by a severe and unrelenting discipline. The college day began at six in the morning with prayer in the large hall. Classes started promptly at eight and continued till noon; after an interruption for dinner and recreation, students were expected to continue their studies privately in their chambers. Undergraduates wore a uniform coat, waistcoat and breeches of blue-gray, and only the frogs on the buttonholes distinguished one class from another.

A serious young man, John Quincy easily adapted himself

to this atmosphere which must have stifled more pleasure-loving spirits. His mind was on his books, and the few friendships of his college years were, so he said, "only with the best characters in my class . . . with whom I enjoy many social half hours" in literary discussion. He delivered one of the valedictory addresses at the commencement exercises, which was lauded by a newspaper as justifying the public's "preconceived partiality" for the son of Ambassador John Adams.

For the next three years, John Adams read law in the Newburyport offices of Theophilus Parsons, a successful attorney and competent instructor. And now, for the first time, he was caught up in the social whirl of a young men's club in a New England town; his diary of these years is a gay chronicle of dancing and parties, of sleigh rides in the winter and sailing in summer.

At twenty-three Adams opened law offices at Boston. As a fledgling attorney with few clients, John Quincy had much time to ponder his future. His thoughts turned often to politics and to the issues that were already dividing the young nation.

The ending of the Revolutionary War brought with it the end of the unity of purpose which had animated people of all social classes in the common struggle. New conflicts came to the fore. Farmers and merchants, debtors and creditors were at loggerheads. Who would be the beneficiaries of the Revolution, and who would carry the burdens accumulated in that struggle? What shape would the society originating from the Revolution take, and how would it be governed? In the debates over the adoption of the Constitution these questions had already stirred public controversy. Two opposing views began to take shape: one in favor of a government directed by an elite of propertied and educated men, the other in favor of a more democratic society. The French Revolution, a passionate and violent upheaval to settle essentially the same questions, occurred in the midst of this debate and acted as a catalyst to range the people into op-

The Harvard University campus as it looked in John Quincy Adams' student days.

posite camps, and eventually into two rival and antagonistic political parties.

As a law student, John Quincy took no public position in the debate in Massachusetts on the ratification of the Constitution. In private talks with friends, however, he supported the "Anti-Federalists," and he wrote in his diary that the Constitution was "calculated to increase the power, influence and wealth of those who have any already" and that the charter's adoption would "favor the Aristocratic party." His attitude soon changed, however, partly because he saw no good in opposing the decision of the majority, partly because he was influenced by the vigorous Federalist position taken in his father's pamphlet *In Defense of the Constitution*—but mostly, perhaps, because John Quincy, viewing himself as one of the elite who were called upon to govern, was no rebel in his youth.

A few years later, in the summer of 1791, writing under the pseudonym Publicola, John Quincy made his debut in politics defending these altered opinions. The occasion was the publication of a booklet by Thomas Paine, *The Rights of Man*. It was an ardent defense of the French Revolution against a virulent attack by Edmund Burke. Even though Burke was still respected by the American public for his stand against King George's policies in the American Revolution, it was a brash act on the part of young John to oppose Paine, revered by the people for the famous writings which had inspired the struggle for independence. What prompted John Quincy to take sides in the argument was the dispute it disclosed between two men much closer to him than Paine and Burke: In an introduction to Paine's pamphlet, Thomas Jefferson expressed the hope that it would lay low some of the "political heresies" then prevalent in the country. John Quincy interpreted this remark as an oblique criticism of his father's writings and leaped into the fray. By what right, he demanded, did Mr. Jefferson set himself up as a "judge of orthodoxy"? The political views set forth in the Publicola articles were those of a conservative. Publicola exalted the virtues of the English constitution, which he found better suited for an American form of government than the revolutionary doctrines of France.

Publicola's articles raised a storm of controversy. But much of the "torrent of abuse," as John Quincy termed the criticism, was directed not at him but at his father, whom Jefferson, Madison and others believed the author of the essays. Though reprinted in London, Edinburgh and Dublin and translated into Dutch, the articles won John Quincy no popularity at home. He now resolved to establish his position as a lawyer firmly before he ventured again into politics, and a few brief but unhappy excursions into local affairs reinforced this decision. The resolution, however, was to fare no better in the midst of turbulent political developments than the resolution his father had made two decades earlier in a similar situation.

On September 20, 1792, at Valmy, the people's army of revolutionary France repelled the invasion of the combined forces of the monarchies of Europe. An explosion of joy greeted the victory in America. In all the principal towns, masses of people donned the cockade, sang "The Marseillaise," toasted the French Revolution in huge street banquets. They saw in the victory a triumph of the principles of their own revolution, and they demanded that their government should now reciprocate the aid which France had extended to the colonies during the war for independence. Six months later, Edmond Genêt, the new French ambassador, landed in Charleston, South Carolina. His overland journey to Philadelphia, then the capital, was a triumphal procession; the scenes of the Valmy celebrations were repeated by larger numbers and with even greater enthusiasm. On the day Genêt entered the capital, Washington issued a proclamation of neutrality in the European war. A wave of disappointment, and then of anger, spread through the country. At this point John Quincy again entered the lists, once again as a conservative and on Washington's side.

Under the pen name Marcellus, he wrote in a series of

articles which appeared in the *Columbian Centinel* that it was in the interests of the United States to avoid involvement in European wars and that without an army or a navy the country would be incapable of defending its seacoast or its commerce against an English attack. Furthermore, he maintained, the United States was not bound by the 1778 treaty of alliance with France, since the monarch with whom it had been made had since been deposed, and it was not within America's province to determine whether the treaty rights had been inherited by the revolutionary government or by the royalist exiles.

The tide of sympathy for France continued to mount, but it now began to take a peculiarly American political turn. Democratic societies, modeled after the Jacobin clubs in France, sprang up everywhere to give voice to the growing discontent of small farmers and city debtors with the conservative policies of Washington, Hamilton and Adams, who were labeled "monocrats." Jefferson and Madison secretly supported these groups, which were to be the precursors of the Jeffersonian party. Genêt, the impetuous French emissary, threw diplomatic caution to the winds and plunged into the conflict as a partisan.

His imprudent actions and declarations provided John Quincy with another opportunity to take up his political pen. Under the sobriquet of Columbus, he launched a vehement denunciation of Genêt and a warm defense of Washington. It was an outrage, he declared, for this "beardless foreigner," this "petulant stripling," to impugn the reputation of the man who had won the title of "father of his country." The ambassador, he continued, had abused his privileges and the hospitality of the country which had granted them by meddling in domestic affairs, "connecting himself with a particular party of American citizens hostile to the national government of the country," and impugning the country's sovereignty by appeals to the people to reverse the policies of their elected representatives. Nothing could be more "fatal to the liberties of the state" than to permit "the interference of foreigners . . . in the dissensions of fellow-citizens," Columbus concluded, adding that the President had the right to revoke the credentials of a foreign emissary and to demand his recall.

This debate John Quincy won. The Jeffersonians were too embarrassed by Genêt's flagrant acts—he had even defied a government interdiction to license privateers to sail from American ports—to reply effectively. The young man had won more than he knew. For while he was writing his father that many persons "would be more clamorous" in their praise "if they were not disposed to check the writer's aspirations," the articles were attracting attention in the highest places. Washington felt under obligation to the author, his father thought, for "having turned the tide of sentiment against Genêt," and he made discreet inquiries to determine the authorship of the Columbus articles. On May 29, 1794, the President submitted to the Senate the nomination of John Quincy Adams for the post of minister resident to the Netherlands. The nomination was confirmed on the following day.

3

The Making of a Diplomat

"You will see Europe at the most interesting period of its history," wrote John Adams to the fledgling ambassador, not yet twenty-five years old, on the eve of departure for his first diplomatic assignment. The Vice-President was trying to counter his son's lack of enthusiasm for what he expected to be a dull and unrewarding mission. John Quincy was to see his father's words proved true almost from the day he set foot on European soil.

The French Revolution had reached the second stage of its stormy existence. Robespierre had lost his head under the guillotine, as John Quincy learned while passing through London, and the period of terror and internal upheaval had come to an end. More moderate men replaced the Jacobins at the helm of the French government. But if the volcano had subsided in France, its hot lava continued to pour across the frontiers. The crowned heads of Europe had formed a coalition, led by England, to extirpate the revolution, which threatened them with the fate of decapitated Louis XVI. Their combined armies of feudal mercenaries were, however, no match for the democratic battalions of France. The flaming watchwords of "Liberty, Equality, Fraternity" preceded the French armies and aroused the people behind enemy lines to follow the example of France in avenging ancient wrongs.

The Netherlands was on the brink of such a change when John Quincy Adams arrived at The Hague on October 31, 1794, to assume his ambassadorial post. A French army of 70,000 men spearheaded by forces under the command of a Dutch revolutionary general swarmed across the Belgian frontier into Holland. The country was virtually defenseless. The tiny Dutch army refused to fight; the Austrians and the Prussians beat a quick retreat and withdrew their troops from the country. Resistance was left entirely to the English, whom the Dutch people detested for their plunder and arrogance. The reigning Prince of Orange was equally disliked. His aristocratic regime owed its survival against a democratic opposition almost entirely to the British. The young American ambassador quickly realized the extent of this dependence. "When I first arrived," he wrote to John Adams, "I was surrounded with that sort of malevolence which a West India faithful African may be supposed to bear to the enemy of his master. . . . It was shown in the whole hierarchy of servitude, from the President of the States General to the hairdresser. . . ."

Events soon put an end to this unpleasantness—and to those responsible for it. On the 27th of December, the French armies under General Pichegru attacking all along the line caught their antagonists by surprise by crossing the frozen Waal. The coalition forces were in full retreat, led by the English, who drew back across the Rhine. Without awaiting the arrival of the French, the Dutch patriots rose in revolution and ousted the officials of the old regime in all the major cities. Foreseeing the outcome, the Statdholder hired a fishing boat and, together with the rest of the royal family, slipped off in the dark of night to an English haven. John Quincy marveled at the peacefulness of the revolution and the discipline of the French troops. There was a great deal of shouting, commotion and enthusiasm in the streets as the tree of liberty was planted, but relatively little violence. Even the Dutch were amazed at the severity with which French soldiers were punished for the slightest act of plunder, drunkenness or disorder; never had a foreign army behaved in so exemplary a fashion in their country. "We come not as conquerors but as brothers," the French proclaimed as their armies advanced. "The persons, property, customs and beliefs of the people will be respected; the troops will pay for their supplies. . . ."

Most of the diplomatic corps, among them the ministers of Great Britain, Spain, Prussia and Sardinia, withdrew as the French armies approached. But the Portuguese and Russian ministers, the ambassadors of Sweden, Denmark, and Poland, and John Quincy Adams remained and were treated with great deference. The warmest reception was reserved for the American ambassador. The new leaders of the Batavian Republic, as the Netherlands was now renamed, were old and stalwart friends of the United States. They had been enthusiastic supporters of the American revolution and had insisted that the Stadthoider, despite his fears of antagonizing the British, recognize the new American republic. Dutch bankers had extended generous loans. Pieter Paulus, the new Batavian president, had been a warm friend of John Adams during his first mission to Holland in 1782, and he told John Quincy that he remembered him as a boy. He was eager, he told the ambassador, to renew and consolidate the ties of his government with the United States. John Quincy Adams returned these gestures of good will by remaining in official capacity at The Hague and thus extending American recognition to the Batavian Republic.

Adams was treated with equal cordiality by the representatives of France. They stressed the common revolutionary origin which bound the two countries in ties of friendship. They understood, they said, America's position of neutrality and would do nothing to embarrass it and everything to encourage trade between the two countries. Demands made by

The French army, spearheaded by forces under the command of a Dutch revolutionary general, marched across the Belgian frontier to occupy Holland.

the American ambassador, respecting the rights, properties and vessels of Americans, were expedited with dispatch.

An honored guest at the dinner tables of the victorious French generals, John Quincy learned the secrets of the invincibility of their armies. Inspired by the justice of their cause, the soldiers were prepared to undergo great hardships, to fight all day and if the enemy was not beaten to sleep in the fields and resume the fight the next morning. The officers, often drawn from the ranks or from humble condition, shared the lot of the troops, whom they commanded directly from the field rather than from safe positions miles behind the front line. Adams was learning of the great revolution in the art of war which has endured down to modern times.

These signs were promising, but Adams, skeptical of popular revolutions, was quick to see the flaws in the new Dutch regime. The French, he noted, had come as liberators but had remained as conquerors. Holland was weak and defenseless, its navy only a glorious memory, its commerce ruined by the wars; it had gained the forms of independence but in reality had become a vassal of France. When the French demanded large reparations and the cession of territory as an indemnity for Holland's participation in the war on the side of the feudal coalition, the ardent Dutch supporters of the French Republic leading the Batavian government cried out that the principles of the French Revolution were being violated. With unabashed cynicism Sieyès, the French representative, replied that while the French may have proclaimed the *theory* of the sovereignty of all nations, *in practice* they were concerned only with the sovereignty of the French nation. Principles, he added, are for the schools; states are concerned with interests.

The new foreign policy of the French Republic, a combination of revolution and conquest, was to demolish the feudal system in Europe, although in the end it would undermine also the French Revolution. Repelled by this seeming duplicity, Adams became a staunch opponent of any policy of American friendship with France in the fear—somewhat unfounded because of the immense distance that separated the two countries—that the United States would suffer the fate of Holland. These were private thoughts and opinions he transmitted in diplomatic correspondence with the Secretary of State and the Vice-President. In practice, however, there was little for him to do beyond processing American loans to Dutch bankers. "An American Minister at the Hague," he complained to his father, "is one of the most useless beings in creation." In effect, he continued, he is nothing but a reporter, and a man must have "a degraded idea of himself, who can be satisfied with the part of receiving the pay of a nation for the purpose of penetrating the contents of a newspaper."

John Adams had a different opinion of his son's work and he wrote him of "the pleasure I have received from the satisfaction you have given the President [Washington] and the Secretary of State [Randolph] . . . from the clear, comprehensive and masterly accounts . . . of the public affairs of the nations in Europe, whose situations and politics it most concerns us to know. Go on, my dear son . . . continue to deserve well of your father, but especially of our country."

The respect John Quincy had won soon earned him a new assignment, more exciting but also more dangerous. In August of 1795, Thomas Pickering, the new Secretary of State, on the advice of Washington, instructed John Quincy Adams to proceed to London and exchange ratifications of the Jay Treaty and to continue negotiations regarding some disputed points in the treaty. Adams had been chosen for the task because John Jay had left London for the United States and Thomas Pinckney, the ambassador to England, was in Madrid on diplomatic business. It was stipulated, however, that if Adams could not get to London before October 20, the treaty was to be signed by William Deas, Pinckney's private secretary. Due to the slowness of the mails, John Quincy did not receive his instructions until October 19.

A series of mishaps detained him in Holland until October 31. Too late to fulfill his mission, John Quincy still decided to proceed.

Jay's Treaty, championed by Washington, Hamilton and John Adams, was the subject of violent political discord in the United States. To close the holes in its blockade of France and thus starve its enemy into submission, England began a systematic attack on neutral shipping bound for France and much of it that was bound for other destinations. Hundreds of American vessels were seized, and the deadly threat to American commerce brought the two countries to the brink of war. The intent of the supporters of the treaty was to save American shipping and avoid a war. Their Jeffersonian opponents, however, claimed that the pact was a surrender of the principles of neutrality proclaimed by Washington himself during the Genêt affair and a violation of the treaty of friendship with France. Furthermore, Jay had been worsted during the negotiations and England had got the better of the bargain. The treaty was highly unpopular in the United States; Hamilton was stoned while attempting to defend it.

The one virtue John Quincy Adams saw in the treaty was that it averted a war, and he had explained this to Jay in London a year before. To affix his signature to the pact seemed like signing his own political death warrant, and it was only out of a sense of duty to his country and of loyalty to his father that he had accepted the mission. However, once the treaty had been signed in his absence, John Quincy must have seen himself in a new role. If in further negotiations he succeeded in modifying some of the most obnoxious features of the agreement, it would become more palatable to the American public; he would make his mark as a diplomat and render an important service to the hard-pressed Federalists. The idea was well conceived, but he did not reckon with the diplomatic skill and cunning of his British hosts.

When he first arrived in London, it appeared to John Quincy that the British attitude had altered from the frigid and barely civil treatment they had accorded his father as America's first ambassador to the Court of St. James's some ten years earlier. But the display of cordiality, at first pleasing to the young man, was so excessive that it could not but awaken his suspicions. In a subtle appeal to his political and personal loyalties, an attempt was made to persuade Adams that his friends (Washington, Hamilton, his father) were Britain's friends, and his "enemies" (Jefferson, Madison, Monroe) were also Britain's enemies. The unspoken conclusion was that Britain's interests were America's interests. The other gambit was an appeal to John Quincy's vanity. He was told that Deas had a thoroughly disagreeable personality and that the British hoped Pinckney, the ambassador, would be recalled and that Adams would take his place.

Instead of being lured, Adams was quick to resent these stratagems. "What sort of a soul does this man suppose I have?" he asked himself. To Hammond (the man in question), British Under Secretary for Foreign Affairs, he replied that the controversy in the United States was a family quarrel and that the men whom Hammond had called enemies were as much Americans to Adams as were his political friends. But the second device of the British was to prove more embarrassing, and Adams's attempt to extricate himself placed him in a somewhat ludicrous situation. He was suddenly confronted with the official announcement describing him as "Minister Plenipotentiary" to England, the position actually held by Pinckney. Instead of concentrating on the issues that had brought him to London, Adams was deflected into protests requesting that his title be corrected to "Minister-Resident at The Hague." The British soon realized that he was not their man, and Adams got absolutely nowhere with Lord Grenville, the Foreign Secretary, in his attempt to adjust points of dispute such as neutral rights and the impressment of American seamen. The crowning insult was the publication of an official notice of Adams's impending departure even before he himself had made plans to leave.

The English mission was a bitter experience for young Adams, and to some extent it deflated his supreme self-confidence. "I have been accustomed all my life," he wrote his father, "to plain dealing and candor, and am not sufficiently versed in the arts of political swindling to be prepared for negotiating with a European Minister of State." But the lasting impression of his visit, which would influence all his future thinking on foreign policy, was contained in these words: "Between the United States and Great Britain no *cordiality* can exist. I do not think it is on our part to be desired. But peace may, and I hope will, continue, notwithstanding all the conspiracies that have been formed against it in America and Europe."

Despite Adams's disappointment, the English mission would stand out as the high point of his first years in the foreign service. He had passed the test for a diplomat. By playing on his youth and ambition with flattery and favors, by encouraging his suspicions of his father's political antagonists, an attempt had been made to mold him into a pliable instrument of British policy. Others, and more experienced men, had succumbed to this treatment before—at the hands of both the British and the French. In resisting the temptation to put self and partisanship over what he considered his duty, John Quincy Adams had given the first example of that remarkable personal integrity which was to be the hallmark of his long political career.

Back at The Hague, John Quincy fretted over the time he had wasted on idle amusement in London, at social functions, seeing plays at the famous Drury Lane Theatre, visiting museums, and—although he makes no mention of the fact—meeting Louisa Catherine Johnson, the daughter of the American consul and the woman who would soon be his wife. Resolved to mend his ways, he set himself a strict schedule, which is recorded as follows in his diary:

John Quincy and Louisa Johnson Adams at the time of their marriage.

"Rise and dress at six. Read works of *instruction* [Adam Smith's *Wealth of Nations,* etc.] till nine. Breakfast. Read the papers and translate from the Dutch till eleven or twelve. Then dress for the day. Write letters or attend to other business that occurs between two and three. Walk till half-past three. Dine and sit till five. Read works of *amusement* [Pope's translations of Homer, Dryden's translations of Virgil, and the *Metamorphoses* of Ovid, which Adams translated himself] between eight and nine. Walk again about an hour. Then take a slight supper and my segar, and retire to bed at eleven."

Not long after his return to the Batavian Republic, Adams was reassigned as minister plenipotentiary to Portugal, a promotion which doubled his salary of $4,500. Returning to London to marry Louisa Johnson and await instructions for his new position, he discovered a disconcerting change of plans. John Adams had in the meantime been elected President to replace the retiring Washington, and he was obliged to alter his son's assignment from Lisbon to Berlin. John Quincy was outraged at receiving an appointment from his own father, and he wrote his mother that he would rather have no position at all than expose his father and himself to the charge of nepotism. At this John Adams exploded. Did not the sons of Presidents have the same claim to the benefits of the law as other citizens? "It is," he wrote, "the worst found opinion I have ever known you to conceive. . . ." But it was Abigail Adams who overcame her son's scruples when she forwarded a letter from George Washington which said in part that *"Mr. Adams is the most valuable public character we have abroad, and . . . there remains no doubt in my mind that he will prove himself the ablest of all our diplomatic corps. . . . The country would sustain a serious loss if [his talents and worth] were to be checked by over delicacy on your [John Adams's] part."*

Unfortunately, John Quincy Adams's competent achievement at The Hague ended on an unpleasant note. In the course of his diplomatic correspondence, Adams had made some caustic comments about the dependence of Dutch statesmen on the French government. However immoderate, these remarks were made in confidence and were distinctly not intended for publication. The Federalist Secretary of State, Pickering, thinking to score a point against his political opponents, made them available to the Senate along with other state papers, and the news quickly found its way, with inevitable distortions, into the newspapers. William Vans Murray, John Quincy's successor at The Hague and later one of his most intimate correspondents, wrote that the Dutch were so indignant that they would have demanded Adams's recall had he "not been out of reach of their anger."

After an especially rough voyage by sea and land, Adams, his bride and his brother Thomas arrived at the Prussian capital on November 7, 1797. The ambassador's instructions were limited to a renegotiation of the Treaty of Amity and Commerce signed by the United States and the Kingdom of Prussia in 1785. There were a number of admirable principles in that treaty regarding the rights of neutrals on the high seas which the American government wanted to delete, partly because the war between England and France made their enforcement impossible and partly because the United States in signing the Jay Treaty had already surrendered these principles. Having disapproved of precisely this aspect of the Jay Treaty, Adams consented to proceed only on the grounds that the omission was necessary because of the failure of other powers to recognize these principles of neutrality, not because of any alteration in American policy to serve its own material interests. Adams was favorably impressed by a proposal of the Prussian foreign minister, Haugwitz, that the United States join with other neutral powers (principally the countries of northern Europe) to insist that the belligerents respect their rights. Pickering thoroughly disapproved of the idea. He wrote Adams that such a pact was inconceivable because it could only be directed against England, upon whose navy alone depended "the safety of the portion of the civilized world not yet subjugated by France."

The brusque, impatient tone in Pickering's letter reflected the passions of the great debate between Federalists and Jefferson's Republicans. As neither side yet favored involvement in the war, the question was toward which nation, England or France, America's neutrality would lean. Both countries were attempting to sway the decision in their own favor. The scales were tipped on England's side when the Senate ratified Jay's Treaty by a bare two-thirds majority. But as the majority of the American people were clearly opposed to the treaty, the French hoped that Jefferson's election in 1796 would lead to a reversal of American policy. When instead a two-vote plurality in the electoral college gave the Presidency to John Adams, the French turned to more forcible means to protect their interests. A decree of the French Directory declared that all vessels bearing cargo for England were legitimate prizes of war, and French privateers fell upon American shipping with a greater vengeance than even Britain had done before the signing of the Jay Treaty. Diplomatic relations were virtually ruptured when the French government refused to accept Pinckney's credentials as American ambassador to replace James Monroe, who had been recalled by Washington on the grounds of partiality to the French. A final attempt to resolve the differences between the two countries resulted in the disgraceful XYZ Affair, and the American commission in Paris was treated with insufferable insolence and contempt. The United States stood on the brink of war with France.

John Quincy was thousands of miles from the scene where the issue was being decided, but his position in scores of letters, official and unofficial, was fiercely partisan. The French Revolution, he held, was a menace to the integrity and sovereignty of the United States. Its aims were to overthrow the constituted government and to impose a puppet regime similar to those in the European nations it had conquered. "The French party," as he dubbed the Anti-Federalists, was composed of naive men, fools or knaves, who in the end would meet the fate of their counterparts in Europe. His contempt for men like Monroe and Thomas Paine was unbounded; only Jefferson was spared the sting of his vitriolic pen. All of this was a far cry from the view he had expressed to a friend on returning from London when he wrote, "If I do not look upon them [the French] as the first people on the face of the globe, it is only because *I have a country*." Now for the first time Adams was prepared to jettison the policy of neutrality, which he had previously considered the keystone of America's foreign relations and the *sine qua non* for its existence as an independent nation. He urged the arming of merchant ships, the building of a navy, and preparations for what he considered an unavoidable war with France.

The United States was in the midst of feverish preparations for war when John Quincy received an unexpected message from his friend at The Hague. Murray related a conversation with the French minister, Pichon, in which the latter told him that "a great change had taken place in the mind of his government on American affairs, and it was now clear to them they had been deceived by men on both sides of the water. . . . He stated over and over . . . the interests which France has in not going to war with us . . . urging, pressing a negotiation."

Adams at first believed this was a ruse occasioned by military reverses the French had suffered. But in the succeeding months, the attitude of the French government confirmed its good will and sincerity. There was no doubt that France wanted peace with the United States and was now prepared to deal with American emissaries on a basis of equality. In John Quincy's opinion this change in policy resulted from America's firm resistance and from the fact that French shipping had virtually been driven off the high seas, with enormous losses in ships and men. President Adams in Washington was now determined to accept the olive branch proffered by the French government. His decision wrecked the Federalist party and destroyed his own chances for reelection as President, but it led to a satisfactory and enduring peace with France.

The Federalists, led by Hamilton, had staked their political future on a war with France. Some of them John Quincy believed were under "English influence," although he had previously scoffed at the idea of an "English Party" in the United States. Others counted upon using the war for the partisan purpose of smashing their political opponents; the infamous Alien and Sedition Acts were enacted partly with that end in view. But John Adams was cut from a different cloth. Much as he detested the equalitarian doctrines of "revolutionary Jacobinism," he refused to permit his dislike of the French form of government to determine the nation's foreign policy. A war with France, once America's principal grievances has been remedied, might have jeopardized the nation's independence by making it completely dependent on the protection of the British navy. It was precisely to avert such dangers, Adams believed, that Washington had promulgated the principle of noninvolvement in Europe's wars, which could now be served only by peace with France. The Farewell Address was an article of faith for President Adams; and although he had vigorously prepared for war and had signed the sedition law—which he later regretted—he refused to allow partisan interests to stand in the way of his duty of reasserting Washington's creed in the changed circumstances.

"You have given the most decisive proof," John Quincy wrote his father upon learning of his defeat in the elections of 1800, "that you were the man not of any party but of the whole nation." That description would apply in the years to come to the son as well. Both men, in fact, in attempting to serve the nation as a whole, suffered more at the hands of their political friends than at those of their enemies.

The decline in his father's political fortunes temporarily put an end to John Quincy's career. In a moment of bitterness at his betrayal and defeat in the election, John Adams recalled his son from Berlin rather than give his successor that satisfaction. Jefferson, a lifelong friend, had not the slightest intention of removing John Quincy Adams. But the deed was done, and with his wife and baby son, George Washington Adams, John Quincy returned to America and to a new political career.

4

*The Young Senator
from Massachusetts*

RETURNING HOME in the fall of 1801 after seven years' absence, John Quincy Adams found America greatly changed in appearance. "I find everywhere," he wrote, "the marks of peace within our walls, and prosperity within our palaces—for palaces they may truly be called, those splendid and costly mansions which since my departure seem to have shot up from the earth by enchantment."

The new affluence which John Quincy noted was the outward sign of the benefits the young republic was enjoying from the treaty with France, which had cost John Adams his political career, and from the approaching truce in Europe's wars which Napoleon would impose on England. No longer molested by hostile navies, the sailing vessels of New England were crowding those of old England for maritime primacy, and the prosperity of American commerce brought increasing wealth to the nation's farms and infant industries.

The changes in the political landscape were equally imposing. A virtual revolution had driven the Federalists from the field they had dominated uninterruptedly for the past twelve years. Jefferson was in the White House, and his Republicans commanded majorities in both houses of Congress and in thirteen of the sixteen state legislatures. "The power of the administration," John Quincy noted, "rests upon a stronger majority of the people throughout the Union than the former administrations ever possessed."

Massachusetts was one of the last holdouts of Federalism. Still living on its past glories, refusing to adjust itself to the changing trends in the country, the party was headed by a group of die-hards led by Timothy Pickering, whose hatred of Jefferson and his policies was almost irrational. Because of his French treaty, John Adams was marked as a "traitor," and the same treatment would soon be visited upon the son. He like his father belonged to the more moderate if weaker wing of the party.

John Quincy had resumed his law practice but his restless thoughts returned to politics. He wanted to be, however, not "the man of a party" but "the man of my whole country." The lure of the political arena was too strong for him to remain out of it for long, and in 1802 he ran for a seat in the Massachusetts State Senate. He asserted his independence almost from the first day in office with a motion to allow the Republican minority proportional representation on the legislative council. Soon thereafter he opposed the chartering of a state bank because control was vested in the hands of Boston's wealthy Federalists. The party regulars considered him unmanageable. "This man," said one of them, "is not our friend, but against us," while another was more vitriolic: "Curse on the stripling, how he apes his sire!"

In the fall of that year John Quincy entered the Congressional elections and was defeated by about fifty votes. Three months later, however, he was elected to the United States Senate. The two Massachusetts seats in the upper chamber had become vacant at the same time. In the contest that followed in the state house of representatives, the Adams faction won the senior post with a full six-year term for John Quincy, while the junior Senatorship went to Pickering, who was a good twenty years older than his colleague—another slight for which the young man would never be forgiven.

Adams arrived at Washington in the midst of an event of momentous significance for the American nation. Napoleon had offered to sell the entire Louisiana territory, and President Jefferson had agreed to buy it for $15,000,000—828,000 square miles at three cents an acre! It was a real estate transaction which in scope and price would be unparalleled in history. Even more important at the time was the fact that in removing a powerful and potentially dangerous neighbor from American soil, the purchase had eliminated a base for foreign empire, a source of friction for Mississippi River trade and a possible cause of future wars.

Great was the rejoicing in Washington. Only Jefferson, who had initially bargained merely for New Orleans and the Floridas, had sober moments of reflection. There was no provision in the Constitution for the acquisition of territory, either by purchase or conquest, nor for the procedure to be followed to absorb the peoples involved into the Union. A major precedent fraught with grave consequences for the future of the Union and the relationship between the Federal government and the states was about to be established. Jefferson considered the possibility of an amendment to the Constitution that would encompass the admission of new territory. But the idea was a dangerous one. The first consul, soon to be emperor of the French, had acquired Louisiana from the Spanish by an agreement which he had not kept. He had sold it to the United States to prevent it from falling into the hands of the English, with whom he was again at war. An unexpected turn of the wheel of fortune might cause him to change his mind. There was no time to be lost over constitutional questions, and Jefferson dropped his plan for an amendment.

The young Senator from Massachusetts warmly supported the acquisition of Louisiana; he voted for the appropriations necessary for its purchase and even attended a Republican banquet to celebrate the victory. This was the first rupture in a widening schism with his Federalist colleagues. In his disappointment over the Republican victory in the elections of 1800, Adams had written from Berlin to his friend Murray on hearing the rumors of the retrocession of Louisiana to the French: "Let them [the French] take Louisiana!" But as a Senator, the idea of placing party and sectional interests over those of the nation was inconceivable to him. The Essex Junto had no such scruples. This hard-core group of Federalists feared that the purchase not only would add to Jefferson's popularity, but would pave the way for the eventual entry of a group of states with rival political interests. They saw their hopes for a return to power doomed by any change in the tenuous balance of power. Opposing the treaty to a man, they reserved their greater venom for John Quincy. "He will certainly be denounced and excommunicated from the party," wrote a Worcester newspaper.

Senator Adams, however, had not accepted the administration's position uncritically. Unaware of the President's private opinions on the Constitutional problem, he revived Jefferson's project for a Constitutional amendment. He told the Senate that while overriding national interest justified the purchase, the United States had no legal writ to enable it to annex the people of the territory without their approval or to tax them without their consent. Except for a few Federalist votes contemptuously offered in favor of Adams's resolutions, his politically unassailable position found no support in the Senate. Some time later, Adams sponsored another Constitutional amendment to allay the fears of his constituents at the admission of states carved from the Louisiana territory that would weight the balance in Congress heavily in favor of the South and slavery. To Adams, slavery was both immoral and dangerous for the Union. He proposed, however, to abolish not slavery but the three-fifths rule which had been written into the Constitution as a compromise. It gave the slaveowners three additional votes for every five slaves they owned. By annulling the rule, the North would gain in the House, where representatives were elected by population, while the South would gain in the Senate by the addition of Louisiana Purchase states. The amendment found little favor either in Congress or in the state legislatures, and it was soon forgotten.

While still a Senator, Adams was appointed Boyltson Professor of Rhetoric and Oratory at Harvard. None of his appointments had pleased him more, and he planned to settle down to a teaching career when his term of office expired. But the unpredictable course of world events soon prevented Adam's contemplated—but never realized—retirement from politics.

Clouds of war over Europe once again began to menace the United States. In 1806, after his brilliant victories at Austerlitz and Jena, Napoleon entered Berlin in triumph. He was now master of all Europe up to the frontiers of the Russian empire. The one flaw in his conquest was Britain's continued rule of the seas, which Nelson's famous naval victory at Trafalgar confirmed beyond question. The war was thus restricted for a time to the economic front, where each side sought to paralyze the other's trade and thus starve its enemy into submission. The neutral nations, particularly the United States, were caught in the middle of this titanic struggle.

At first the United States profited from the war. Its ships became the major carriers of West Indian produce, particularly from the French possessions, to the ports of Europe. Jealous of her overseas maritime competitor and alarmed at the consequences of this trade, Britain employed the full force of her naval power to restrict American shipping. The notorious Rule of War of 1756, which in effect prohibited trade with other nation's colonies, was reinvoked. British warships lay in wait outside American ports to seize any ships engaged in this "contraband" traffic. The final outrage was an unprovoked attack upon an American man-of-war, the *Chesapeake*, just off the Virginia capes, causing death and injury to American sailors.

The United States was in a critical position. The country had no naval power with which to defend its commerce and was totally unprepared for war. But to submit to Britain's arrogant demands would be a blow to America's dignity as an independent nation from which she might never recover. Jefferson resorted to every expedient short of war. He sent a mission to London to negotiate the dispute, while Congress strengthened his hand by voting the Non-Importation Act, forbidding the entry of British manufactures into American ports. Both measures failed; in fact, Britain expanded its interdictions by decreeing that neutral vessels entering unblockaded ports on the Continent were obliged, under penalty of seizure, to secure a British license and to pay a tax on their cargoes. Napoleon retaliated in his Berlin and Milan decrees, which declared prizes of war all ships which had submitted to British search or had paid the tax. Faced with a massive seizure of American vessels, Congress ordered an embargo on all American trade with belligerent ports.

The seaboard states, and particularly New England, resented the loss of commerce resulting from these measures. John Quincy Adams was the only New England man to stand against the tide. His was the sole Federalist vote in the Senate for the Non-Importation Act. When the *Chesapeake* was attacked, he joined in a meeting of public indignation with the Republicans at Boston, a meeting which the Federalists boycotted. He was the chairman of the committee which drafted the Embargo Act. "This measure," he told a colleague, "will cost you and me our seats, but private interests must not be put in opposition to public good." "Apostate," "turncoat," "popularity seeker," "party scavenger" were some of the words of abuse flung at him in the Federalist newspapers. John Quincy calmly replied that the men who wanted to submit to Britain's demands were like the old "tories." He said that their course would end in the surrender of American independence and that he had refrained from urging a declaration of war in fear that the tories would seize the occasion to initiate a civil war behind the lines. But the die was cast. John Quincy Adams knew it, and so did his father, who wrote the Senator in January 1808:

"You are supported by no party; you have too honest a heart, too independent a mind, and too brilliant talents, to be sincerely and confidentially trusted by any man who is under the domination of party maxims or party feelings. . . . You may depend upon it that your fate is then decided. . . . You ought to know and expect this, and by no means to regret it."

John Adam's forebodings were not exaggerated. The following May, Pickering took his revenge by forcing an election for Senator in the Massachusetts House of Representatives six months before it was scheduled. John Quincy Adams was narrowly defeated by a vote of 248 to 213. When the state legislature voted to instruct its senators to vote for the repeal of the Embargo Act, John Quincy resigned his seat immediately. "I could not," he wrote a friend, "consistently with my principles continue for a moment longer the representative of a body of men whose policy was so utterly abhorrent to what I conceive the sacred duty of every *independent American*."

His political enemies pursued him remorselessly into his private life. While there is no indication of any attempt to undermine his law practice, there was a deliberate and public campaign to discredit him as a teacher at Harvard. Fortunately, the majority of his students, Adams noted gratefully, could not be convinced that he was "an ignorant [impostor] in literature" even though "they were made to believe that I was a sort of devil incarnate in politics (about which I could not talk to them)."

A "devil" to some, others held him in higher esteem than ever. Although a private citizen, John Quincy continued to influence foreign policy decisions through correspondence with Republican friends in Congress. His political alignments had changed but he declined, despite Republican urging, to run again for public office.

On March 4, 1809, James Madison was inaugurated President. One of his first acts in office was to offer John Quincy the ambassadorship at St. Petersburg. The offer was accepted. John Quincy Adams would resume his diplomatic career at the Court of the Czar of All the Russias, where he had begun it twenty-eight years earlier.

5

St. Petersburg Welcomes Ambassador Adams

ALEXANDER I succeeded to the Russian throne in 1801, when his father, Paul I, was assassinated by a conspiracy of nobles in which Alexander was indirectly involved. Cultured, affable and charming in manner, the young czar was torn between the democratic ideas he had absorbed as a boy from his radical Swiss tutor and the preservation of the absolute autocracy over which he ruled. His reign began with great projects of reform, such as the emancipation of the serfs and the establishment of constitutional government; it ended in stark reaction which cast its shadows over the New World as well as Europe.

It was during an interim between these two periods that John Quincy Adams arrived at the Russian capital. Alexander had shelved his plans for reform—temporarily, he believed—for dreams of world conquest. Two years earlier, in 1807, Alexander had signed a treaty with Napoleon at Tilsit. Its secret stipulations provided for Russian expansion into Finland and Turkey. Six months later the French emperor was urging the czar to join him in an expedition through Persia and Afghanistan for the conquest of India. But the consequence of this alliance was an English declaration of war and the resulting restriction of Russian trade. In this situation, the arrival of an American ambassador was particularly welcome, for the czar's advisers believed that, whatever their other differences, the United States and Russia had a common interest in circumventing the British blockade. Adams's instructions from the Department of State confirmed this assumption.

Adams was given a royal reception. The doors of the Russian court were opened wide to him, and everywhere he met with cordiality and respect. It was a new and flattering experience for an American minister to be treated with the same deference as the princes, counts and dukes who constituted the rest of the diplomatic corps. He was presented almost at once to Alexander, and a cordial relationship developed between the two men as they met at court functions and sometimes informally in their morning walks. Invitations to official receptions, balls, and diplomatic dinners showered down upon the Adamses. They marveled at the pomp and splendor of Russian society—the opulent dinners, the lavish homes in town and country, the sparkling diamonds and the regal attire—but they groaned at the strain it placed on the modest salary of an American diplomat. At one point Adams wrote his mother that he was being ruined by the very minimum expenses of maintaining a home and all the servants required to run it.

One of Adams's first diplomatic achievements was to obtain the intercession of the czar for the release of almost two score American ships taken by the Danes as war prizes. Denmark had been caught in a terrible vise between the two warring giants. First the cannon of English warships had leveled Copenhagen, the capital city, and now France was creating economic havoc by constraining Denmark to enforce the blockade against British and neutral shipping. The Danes grasped at the offer of Russian protection. The release of the American ships, however, unleashed a chain of events far beyond Adams's calculations. It proved to be the first major breach in Napoleon's Continental System, which had been intended to ring all of Europe from the Baltic to the Mediterranean with a barrier excluding British products. Other American ships now braved the northern waters, and then came British vessels disguised as American merchantmen. The czar closed his eyes to the traffic, or he accommodated Napoleon's furious protests by token gestures of compliance. This was part of a ruthless game of diplomatic poker between the two emperors, who were now at sword's point over many issues other than the Continental System.

At a chance meeting in March 1812, Alexander confided his apprehensions to Adams: "And so it is that, after all, war is coming. He [Napoleon] keeps on advancing. He began by taking Swedish Pomerania—now he has just occupied Prussia —he can't advance much further without attacking us." A few months later the czar's predictions would materialize. On June 25, Napoleon's legions marched across the Russian border to wage their fatal campaign. The Grand Army conquered their ragged and untrained Russian foe, who were more a horde than an army, but they were conquered in turn by what Adams called "General Famine and General Frost." Their lines overextended, far from their base of supplies in a barren Russian countryside, the French did not reach Moscow until winter, and Moscow burned under their feet.

Adams watched the great retreat from his vantage point in St. Petersburg, as, years before from The Hague, he had observed the rise of the French Eagle. He had predicted the advent of a military dictator from the turmoils of the French Revolution. In a letter to his mother, he commented that Napoleon was an "extraordinary man," and he wondered "whether his niche in the temple will be in line with Alexander [The Great], Caesar and Charlemagne, or with Hannibal, Pompey and Charles the Twelfth of Sweden." As Napoleon and the battered remnants of the Grand Army limped back across Europe, he wrote again to Abigail Adams that "the career of Napoleon's conquests is at an end. . . . A new era is dawning on Europe." Napoleon's defeat he at-

In 1807, Alexander I, Czar of Russia, signed a treaty with Napoleon at Tilsit.
Five years later, Napoleon's army invaded Russia.

tributed in part to the unexpected loyalty of the Russian serfs who, unlike the peasants elsewhere in Europe, had failed to rise against their masters in sympathy with the oncoming French battalions. Adams did not know that these were the only serfs whom Napoleon, for some unknown reason still pondered by historians, did not promise freedom and a share in the estates of their dispossessed masters.

But as the "new era" approached in Europe, hostilities between the United States and England erupted in war. For seven years American Presidents had dodged and parried England's blows, tolerating insult and humiliation in the hope that a turn of events in Europe would bring England to reason. Now at the very worst moment, Adams brooded, when England's formidable enemy was crashing to the ground, this dreaded war had finally come.

6

The "Unnecessary" War of 1812

THE UNDERLYING cause of the War of 1812 was Great Britain's attitude toward its former colonies in North America. Although defeated in the Revolutionary War, England stubbornly refused to be reconciled to the independence and sovereignty of the new American nation. Empires die hard. Britain was setting a pattern of behavior for other nations whose colonies would win their freedom in succeeding generations. England's rulers dreamed of the day they would restore their empire in America. That day would come when their hands ceased to be tied by the wars in Europe. Meanwhile they were determined to punish the obstreperous and ill-bred Yankees who dared to insist upon their neutrality and to pursue an independent foreign policy. "The disposition to chastise us," wrote John Quincy Adams, "has been the constant object of English *power* from the time that James the First chastised the founder of Virginia, Sir Walter Raleigh, and the Puritan founders of New England down to this hour. . . ."

This chastisement had become increasingly more severe and, for the Americans, intolerable. American ships were forced to pay heavy duty and obtain British licenses for cargoes destined for ports outside of the British Isles; large areas of Europe's coastline were declared out of bounds by "paper blockades," and American ships venturing into the prohibited zones were seized as prizes of war. British gunboats insolently rode at anchor within sight of American harbors, searching merchant vessels at gunpoint and forcibly removing thousands of seamen, who were impressed into British service on the pretext that they were "His Majesty's subjects."

Other nations have gone to war for far less cause. If the United States submitted to these indignities through the two administrations of Thomas Jefferson and the one administration of James Madison, it was because no other course seemed open. The country was totally unprepared for war. The nation was divided, with the commercial and wealthiest section, which would have had to finance most of the cost of war, adamantly opposed to hostilities. The New England merchants preferred the lucrative profits that could be made, even after paying the English extortioners, to righting the wrongs of the nation as a whole. Under the circumstances, Jefferson and Madison calculated that they must wait for a turn in the European war unfavorable to England to bring that country to its senses. Meanwhile, trading embargoes were imposed as a substitute for war.

Most men had little faith in this waiting game. Yet, before the middle of 1812, it appeared that these tactics might succeed. Napoleon, through his alliance with Alexander, held all of Europe, excluding the Iberian peninsula, in the palm of his hand. Britain's military problems were compounded by the merciless economic squeeze of the Continental System and the American boycott. Faced with spreading famine and a riotous population, the king's ministers relented, and early in June they proposed the repeal of the Orders in Council. "The embargo of last April," John Quincy wrote his mother, "was applied at the moment when its power was most effectual and was . . . the wrenching stroke to the stubbornness of the British ministers." Thus the major *casus belli* between England and the United States was removed.

Thousands of American seamen were impressed into British service on the pretext that they were "His Majesty's subjects."

That war should have come at the very moment it had become "altogether unnecessary," as Adams said, was due to two other factors, one of them technical and the other political. The first was communications in an age when telephone, telegraph and airplane had not yet been invented, and it took from three to six weeks for a letter to cross the Atlantic even in the swiftest sailing ship. Thus Congress was debating Madison's war message unaware that at the same time the House of Commons was deliberating a major relaxation of its navigation decrees. On June 16, the British parliament annulled the Orders in Council; two days later the American Senate declared war to secure that annulment. Neither legislature was aware of what the other had done.

The second, political, factor was the rise of a party of aggressive nationalists in the years immediately preceding the war. Known as the "war hawks," they were led by Henry Clay and John Calhoun and received strong support in the Western and Southern frontier sections. Although outraged by Britain's attitude, this was not their only motivation. The

Southerners pressed for the annexation of the Spanish Floridas, but the far more strident and belligerent cry was the Western demand for the conquest of Canada. For some of these agitators, the lure was the vast stretches of land that lay to the north, where Indians roamed freely under British protection. Others justified their demands by asserting that a nation had the right to expand to its natural frontiers, a doctrine of the French Revolution. This was most grandiloquently expressed in the winged phrase of a New Hampshire Congressman: "The Author of Nature has marked out our limits in the south, by the Gulf of Mexico; and on the North by the regions of eternal frost." Henry Clay promised an easy victory. In his opinion, a force no greater than the militias of Kentucky was needed "to place Montreal and Upper Canada at your feet." Many of the war party wavered under the slashing tirade of John Randolph: "Go to war," he thundered, "without money, without men, without a navy! Go to war when we have not the courage, while your lips utter war, to levy war taxes! . . . The people will not believe it!" But the frontier Napoleons commanded a majority, and in one of the most divided votes that ever decided an American entry into war, they won the day.

Randolph's predictions were soon confirmed. The war hawks had given the country a policy and a military strategy, but they had provided it with neither an army nor a navy, nor an experienced military staff to carry it out. Under the circumstances, disaster was inevitable. The "drive to the north" petered out into ludicrous comic-opera expeditions. The first thrust into Upper Canada resulted in the capture of the entire American force and the loss of Detroit. The second expedition, from Sackets Harbor and over Lake Ontario, and the third, in the direction of Montreal, were equally catastrophic if slightly less humiliating.

St. Petersburg was in the grip of an Arctic winter when these dismal tidings reached the American ambassador. The Neva was frozen over, snow banks were piled high against the houses, and for seventeen days the temperature had been below zero. It was so cold that, despite the double windows and the heated stoves, John Quincy could hardly hold the pen as he wrote home his melancholy comments on the military events of that winter. Viewing the rout of Frenchmen and Americans in the same winter, he speculated whether it was not "contrary to the course of nature for men of the South to invade the regions of the North. Napoleon should have thought of that. So should the [American] visitors of Upper and Lower Canada." While he believed that a lack of valor was responsible for the American defeat, he was opposed to the acquisition of Canada as an object of the war. "Great Britain is yet too powerful . . . to make it possible for us to retain her remaining possessions at the peace, if we should conquer them by the war. The time is not yet come. . . ."

There was, however, one pale glimmer of hope in the wintry skies of 1812.

The Russians were dismayed by the Anglo-American war. Although they were the allies of England in the war against Napoleon, they depended on the commercial assistance of the United States to offset Britain's maritime supremacy. Hence their interest in ending the hostilities between Britain and America. Acting on behalf of the czar, Chancellor Romanzoff approached the American ambassador with an offer of Russian mediation to settle the transatlantic war. Adams had no instructions from his own government on this point, but rather than lose the opportunity in the months-long delay required for an exchange of letters with Washington, he decided to assume the personal responsibility for agreeing to the Russian offer. His initiative, subsequently approved in Washington, began a chain of events which ultimately led to peace negotiations.

In the face of continuing military reverses, and with little hope for improvement, President Madison seized upon the Russian offer. He dispatched Albert Gallatin, Secretary of the Treasury, and Senator James Bayard to join John Quincy Adams in St. Petersburg to confer with the British. The American commissioners did not arrive in the Russian capital until July 1813. By this time, the British had cooled to the idea of Russian mediation. They had never been enthusiastic about a third party, particularly one with commercial interests in common with the United States, nor did they wish to deal with their former colonies on a footing of equality. And now victories over Napoleon relieved the British of some of their obligations to their Russian allies and provided an excuse to reject the mediation offer. The rejection, however, was forwarded directly to Russian military headquarters in Germany, where the czar, hoping for another change in Britain's attitude, delayed sending the news to St. Petersburg. For six months the American commissioners waited in the Russian capital, and it was not until the snows began to fall again that they learned that they had come halfway across the world on a diplomatic wild-goose chase. Then followed weeks of waiting for instructions from home, for the ice-bound northern seas made communication between Washington and St. Petersburg virtually impossible. As January wore on, Gallatin and Bayard decided to take matters in their own hands, and on a wintry afternoon three horse-drawn sleighs carried them and their baggage out of the Russian capital toward the west.

The American commissioners arrived in London, to learn that the British cabinet, under renewed prodding by Alexander, had had another change of heart and were now ready to engage in direct negotiations with the United States. After much debate, the British finally accepted Gothenburg, Sweden, as the site of the peace parleys. In Washington, Madison appointed a new commission, which included the two envoys already in Europe, Henry Clay, Jonathan Russell, who was the ambassador to Sweden, and John Quincy Adams.

John Quincy was overjoyed at the news of his appointment, which was accompanied by a note from Secretary of State

Monroe offering him, in the event a peace treaty was concluded, the ambassadorship at London. The end of the long
Russian winters was at last in sight. A few weeks later, as he
watched the wild celebration of Napoleon's abdication and
the allied occupation of Paris, his happiness was darkened by
the fear that Britain might now release the full fury of its
military might against the United States. On the morning
of April 28, Louisa Adams, together with little Charles Francis, rode with her husband to the first stage stop at Strelna to
bid him farewell as he went on to Riga.

Arriving at Stockholm on his way to Gothenburg, Adams
learned from Russell that there was still no sign of the British
delegation. A month more was to pass before the American
envoys were informed that the meeting place had been
changed from Sweden to Ghent in Holland. Henry Clay had
already left for the Dutch city when Adams and Russell set
sail from Gothenburg on the *John Adams.*

Adams and his companion reached Holland before the end
of June. John Quincy was delighted to find that the country
"in all its charm" remained "precisely the same as I had last
left it."

The Dutch were even more friendly now toward Americans than they had been during Adams's last visit to Holland.
There were frequent dinners, balls and civic festivities at
which the American envoys were guests of honor; "Hail
Columbia!" was played with great gusto on every possible
occasion. The delegates rented a house which, Adams wrote
his wife, was said to be haunted, although after their entry,
he added, "the perturbed spirits have all forsaken the house
. . . and we hope they are laid forever."

The members of the American delegation were extremely
able and experienced negotiators. Albert Gallatin, of Swiss
origin, was a brilliant, cultured man who had served in the
cabinets of Jefferson and Madison. James A. Bayard, a Senator from Maryland, was charming in manner, capable and
quick-witted. What Henry Clay, the tall, gangling Kentuck-

ian, lacked in polish he more than compensated for by his consummate political realism, a mighty asset at the bargaining table. Adams thought Clay most like himself, with "the same dogmatical, overbearing manner, the same harshness of look and expression. . . . An impartial person judging between [us] I think would say that one has the strongest, and the other the most cultivated understanding; that one has the mind most gifted by nature; and the other a mind less cankered by prejudice. . . ." Jonathan Russell, a competent diplomatic technician, was of lesser political stature than the others and usually looked to Clay for guidance.

By July 6, 1814, with Gallatin's arrival from London, the entire delegation had assembled at Ghent. As the month drew to a close and they continued to wait for the British envoys, a mood of pessimism spread in the group. The omens were bad. A fleet of ships had recently sailed from British ports carrying fifteen thousand veterans of Wellington's campaigns—one flotilla headed for the St. Lawrence River and the other for Bermuda. The London *Times* arrogantly announced: "Our demands may be couched in a single word— Submission!" The American delegates began to wonder if negotiations were possible under such hostile conditions.

The British delegation arrived during the first week of August. Its members were relatively obscure figures in English public life. Admiral Gambier was a dry-land sailor, Dr. William Adams, no relation to John Quincy, an obscure Admiralty lawyer, and Henry Goulburn an undersecretary in the Colonial Office. They were proper British snobs whose outstanding quality was a haughty disdain for Americans. Refusing to dignify the Yankees with a delegation of equals, the British cabinet had sent to Ghent a trio which would receive and transmit the orders from London. The three men referred all questions and proposals to London. In one of his rare moments of humor, John Quincy likened them to the Lord Malmesbury of the French jest: "My lord," said the courtier, "I hope your lordship is well this morning."

"Indeed, sir, I do not know, but I will send a messenger to the court to inquire."

The problem of dealing by remote control with Lord Castlereagh and Lord Bathurst, the heads of the British government, was only one of the difficulties that faced the American commissioners. They had been instructed to negotiate a peace while war was still in progress, which meant they had to retain by diplomatic means the positions that soldiers had failed to hold on the battlefield. Furthermore the two major reasons for America's declaration of war—neutral rights and impressment of seamen—had in effect been eliminated by the nullification of the Orders in Council. It was the British, therefore, who held positions of strength. They were able to take by military means what the Americans refused to grant at the bargaining table. They preferred, however, to gain their ends by bluff and threats, without having to commit troops and money to a campaign across the seas after so many years of exhausting war in Europe. The Americans had no alternative but to call the bluff and to hope that the British would retreat; and if they did not, to pray that the United States would somehow summon the strength to meet the military onslaught. It was a dangerous game that for five long months would try the nerves of the American envoys.

For men of such diverse backgrounds and personalities, remarkable harmony prevailed in the group. Despite their frequent conflicts and disagreements, and flashes of temper in tense and trying circumstances, the five men operated as a team, and their differences were not even suspected by their English counterparts.

The first stage of the negotiations was marked by a British ultimatum demanding, in effect, the dismemberment of the American nation. There were three principal items in these terms:

1. A treaty was to be signed with the Indians on the northwestern frontier which would guarantee their territory against purchase or conquest by either of the two powers.

This would establish a buffer state between the United States and Canada covering an area that would have included one-third of the Union and most of the existing and future states of Ohio, Indiana, Illinois, Wisconsin, and Michigan.

2. The Great Lakes were to be placed under British military occupation. The United States would be permitted the rights of commercial navigation but would be denied the right of maintaining forts, posts or warships on the shores and waters of the lakes.

3. The boundary line from Lake Superior to the Mississippi was to be revised, with Britain retaining her rights of Mississippi navigation, and a revision of the northeastern boundary was to be effected by the cession of an area of Maine to allow a direct route from Halifax to Quebec.

The debate revolved primarily around the first point, because the British had stipulated that the acceptance of the Indian Treaty was the *sine qua non* for the settlement of all other questions. Mr. Goulburn asserted that the Indian barrier was needed to protect British Canada against American ambitions. He claimed that the proclamations of the American commanders at the opening of their ill-fated northern expeditions proved that the annexation of Canada was a war aim of the United States. Fortunately it was Adams and not the war hawk Clay who rebutted these arguments. He brushed aside the contention about Canada with the remark —officially true—that Canada was not an American object of war and that the United States, of course, took no responsibility for the brash pronouncements of its generals. The main point, he contended, was elsewhere. The establishment of the Indian buffer zone demanded by the British doomed a huge expanse of fertile land to remain uncultivated. No treaty, no government and no measure short of extermination could prevent an expanding population—soon to reach 8,000,000 in the United States—from overflowing into this territory, cultivating the soil, building farms and homes and towns. A "bond of paper" that attempted to check human progress and to "exclude posterity from the natural means of subsistence" was not only unworkable, it was "a violation of the laws of nature and of nations." Adams was upholding what may be called the law of civilization over that of original possession. The Indians may have come first and they may have possessed the land for centuries as hunting grounds, but their rights had to yield before a more productive and complicated arrangement of human society. This philosophy would underlie American Indian policy for generations to come. However impressed Mr. Goulburn may have been with Adams's reasoning, the British stubbornly maintained their ultimatum in its original form.

The Americans left the meeting in despair. Bayard noted that the terms were those that the victor imposed on the vanquished. Clay wrote to Monroe that "the prospect of peace has vanished," and Adams, believing that the "tragedy" he had anticipated had come to pass, wrote Louisa to expect his early return to St. Petersburg. Despite the grim outlook, the commission flatly rejected the British terms. They were prepared to conclude fair treaties with the Indians, but they would never surrender the rights to more than one-third of their territory. British demands on the Great Lakes and in the northeast they termed "dismemberment"; and since Britain's proposals were dishonorable, they were therefore completely unacceptable. But they did not break off negotiations, and the next move was up to the British.

Meetings were suspended after the rejection of the British ultimatum. The English envoys urged their government to send the Americans home forthwith. Wiser counsel prevailed in London, where Castlereagh feared that a rupture on the Indian issue would encourage the Americans to launch a more aggressive military campaign and that the break would be wholly beneficial to the Americans. The British yielded slightly on the Indian barrier, but they maintained their demands for unilateral disarmament of the Great Lakes and the revision of the northeast frontier. Adams had written the draft of the first American note, and now Gallatin drafted the second. A refutation of British contentions, point by point, it defiantly declared that this rejection would be maintained even if British arms were successful. "We have rejoined," Adams wrote his wife, "that we do not wish to break off, but we say *no* to their terms. . . . As they have been five days deliberating upon what they shall now say, I concluded that they will finally give us the ball back again, and still contrive to make delay."

Adams was right. The British resubmitted their proposals, which the Americans rejected as obstinately as before. But the more ominous reason for the delay soon became apparent. The British flotilla, which had left in July, sailed up Chesapeake Bay and on August 24 landed a contingent of marines, who scattered the feeble and disorganized resistance and then proceeded into Washington to set fire to the capital city. Adams, who had heard the news in October, reminded his wife that he had written her on the very day of the British landing that "it is impossible the summer should pass without bringing intelligence that will make our hearts ache." He hastened to add, however, that the "misfortune" was but a "trifle" if only it galvanized the fighting spirit of the Americans.

Exulting over their triumph, the British cabinet now issued a new ultimatum to the Americans. They shifted their grounds from the primacy of an Indian buffer zone to explicit demands for territorial aggrandizement. These included their retention of Fort Niagara and Fort Michilimackinac, Moose Island, all the islands in Lake Ontario, and a strip of land running from Fort Niagara to Buffalo on the American side of the Niagara River. Other territorial claims would be added as they were conquered by British arms. Once again the American commissioners put their veto on the new ultimatum, but with the sinking feeling that their actions had little effect in determining the outcome of the war. A new turn of events, however, was soon to alter the course of negotiations at Ghent.

Contrary to expectations, the British "triumph" in Wash-

CULVER PICTURES, INC.

In August, 1814, British forces seized Washington and set fire to the city.

ington aroused only revulsion and contempt throughout Europe. Even in England, the British ministers were on the defensive, trying to justify their action as a retaliation for incendiary deeds of American troops in Canadian cities at the outset of the war. John Quincy was expressing a universal reaction when he wrote that the destruction of the American capital was "contrary to the usages of civilized nations and is without precedent even in the wars of the French Revolution." More than a century would pass before civilized nations would consider this type of "barbarism" an accepted practice of warfare. It did not improve Britain's position in the wrangle for the spoils of victory among the nations meeting at the Congress of Vienna.

An even more critical blow to England's ambitions was delivered on the scene of combat itself. Early in September an imposing force of more than 10,000 redcoats under the command of General George Prevost crossed the Canadian border into New York with Plattsburgh as their destination. A British flotilla sailed into Lake Champlain to clear the way for the advancing infantry. On September 11 they were met by an American naval force under Commodore Thomas Macdonough at Plattsburgh Bay, and in a gun duel which lasted all that Sunday morning, the British men-of-war were sunk to the bottom of the lake. The news of the naval disaster took the heart out of Prevost and, with American militiamen pressing hard on his heels, he ordered a retreat to Canada. Two days later, the campaign which had opened so auspiciously at Washington was halted in its tracks at Baltimore. Their commanding officer dead on the battlefield, and with no reinforcements in sight, the British expedition retreated to waiting ships, which carried them back to Halifax.

These victories put a new edge on the diplomatic weapons of Gallatin and Adams. Lord Bathurst decided to retreat from his previous obstinacy, opening the second stage of the negotiations at Ghent. He instructed his envoys to propose that the Americans draft the terms of a treaty which he promised would receive favorable consideration if they accepted the principle of *uti possidetis* (granting to belligerents the possessions they have won in battle). Unaware of the impact of the reverses at Plattsburgh and Baltimore on their adversaries, the American commissioners viewed Bathurst's new proposal as merely another tactic in the diplomatic war of attrition. Their impressions were reinforced by bad tidings from American agents in London and by rebuffs Gallatin met with in attempting to negotiate loans both at Amsterdam and at Paris.

Nevertheless, the American diplomats rejected the principle of *uti possidetis* out of hand and sat down to the laborious task of drafting their version of the peace terms. Lord Liverpool acidly commented that in denying the unwritten law of possession the Americans were espousing "the extravagant doctrine of some of the revolutionary governments of France, viz., that they will never cede any part of their dominions, even though they shall have been conquered by their enemies." There had been easy unanimity among the Americans on this "extravagant doctrine," but the writing of the treaty was to give rise to long and sometimes acrimonious debates in the delegation.

Gallatin and Adams, assigned to compose the draft, agreed on the main lines of the pact. The rest of the delegation concurred except on two propositions which had no bearing on the causes of the war with England, but now almost produced a private war among the commissioners. In the course of the negotiations, Goulburn had served notice that the British would not renew the right of American fishermen to dry their fish on the Grand Banks of Canada. To alter their position Gallatin proposed to grant the British navigation rights on the Mississippi in return for the fisheries privileges. This precipitated a long and bitter verbal duel between Clay and Adams.

The Kentuckian knew that the granting of the river rights was a mere formality, since the delegation had refused to cede the territory between the British Canadian frontier and the headwaters of the Mississippi. But the very thought of settling the war he had so strongly advocated not only without territorial gains but with the recognition of foreign rights in a Western river seemed a blow aimed directly at his prestige. He lost his temper. How could anyone conceive of equating the river, which represented the nation's future, with the prerogative of "drying fish in the desert"? Besides, he continued, the disloyalty of the New Englanders in the war entitled them to no special consideration, and for his part he would not lend his name to any such transaction.

Adams was just as adamant and almost as emotional. In

addition to his concern for the interests of his section, the
Massachusetts man had a personal attachment to the fisheries
privilege, as John Adams had first wrested it from the British
in the Treaty of 1783. The son would keep his faith with
his father and his state. For two days and nights the argument raged. In the end it was agreed that the Mississippi
need not be mentioned, and the fisheries problem could be
omitted from the treaty because as a component of American independence it required no special recognition.

At this point Adams proposed an alternative based on the
idea that the Americans were in no position to drive a hard
bargain. In place of the treaty, he suggested offering the
British the substitute of restoring the conditions in effect
before the war. Gallatin was enthusiastic about this eminently
realistic view. Bayard was quickly won to it. Clay grumbled
but finally gave his assent, and Russell followed.

While the Americans were wrangling over formulas, a
fateful dialogue was in progress between two men. Lord
Liverpool wrote to the Duke of Wellington in Paris urging
him to take command of the British forces in America. His
acceptance would hold out the hope of a speedy and decisive
victory, which alone would justify a continuation of the conflict to a discontented and war-weary public. The British
general, however, took a dim view of the military prospects
in America, where his reputation might be tarnished for little cause as had been those of other outstanding British officers. Moreover, he wrote, the situation in France, where
Louis XVIII sat on a powder keg of discontent, was too critical to permit his departure to so distant an arena. Declining
Liverpool's invitation, he urged the minister to drop the
principle of *uti possidetis* as untenable in the absence of substantial conquests and to come to terms with the Americans.
Liverpool wrote to Castlereagh that in view of the "unsatis-
factory state of the negotiations at Vienna, . . . the alarming
situation of the interior of France . . . and the state of our
finances," Wellington's refusal to take the American com-

mand left him no choice but to "bring the American war if possible to a conclusion."

Thus the third and final stage of the negotiations at Ghent began with what amounted to an acceptance of Adams's proposal, to which Washington had already given its approval. The British dropped the principle of the right of conquest and made no mention of the Indian buffer state, unilateral control of the Great Lakes or other cessions of territory, but they vetoed, as the Americans expected, the purely ritual articles on impressment, the blockade, amnesty and Indian supervision. The only unresolved questions now were the Mississippi, the fisheries and the Passamaquoddy Islands. "We have everything," wrote Adams, "but peace on our hands." With the end clearly in view, negotiations became more acrimonious. The British envoys, following new instructions that they despised, fought like tigers over trifles and haggled over commas.

Adams was just as relentless. Since you claim Mississippi rights from the Treaty of 1783, he queried, does not your silence on the fisheries privilege connote an American right from the same treaty? Yes! chorused the Englishmen; and then, hearing the echo of their blunder, they shouted, No! If you claim unlimited rights to the Mississippi, Adams pursued, then we shall insist upon unlimited rights to the St. Lawrence. Would it not be better to drop both articles? The British were speechless as Gallatin picked up the attack and Bayard pressed it home. While the Americans waited again for their counterparts to refer to London for advice, Adams commented to his wife that they were dueling with "an adversary who, after demanding empires as an indispensable preliminary falls to playing pushpins for straws."

In the American delegation nerves were frayed, tempers on edge. For four months they had figuratively held their fingers in the dike, and now that the flood had receded they were obliged to battle over nonessentials. The old disagreements erupted. No longer thinking as a diplomat but as a politician who had promised much and gained little, Clay refused to sign the treaty without a clear stipulation against British rights on the Mississippi. Adams countered with an ultimatum regarding New England fisheries rights. With his calm and reasoned manner, Bayard averted the explosion that seemed in the making. The commission then decided unanimously that the Mississippi and fisheries questions would be deferred to negotiations at the end of the war. On another occasion, described by Adams, good-humored banter lightened the tension among the delegates as they were returning from a conference session:

"Mr. Clay remarked that Mr. Goulburn was a man of much *irritation. Irritability,* said I, is the word, Mr. Clay, irritability; and then fixing him with an earnest look, and the tone of voice between seriousness and jest, I added: 'like somebody else that I know.' Mr. Clay laughed, and said, 'Aye, that we do, all know him, and none better than yourself.' And Mr. Gallatin, fixing me exactly as I had done Mr. Clay, said emphatically, 'that is your *best friend.*' 'Agreed,' said I, *'but one.'*—and we passed on in perfect good humor to another topic."

On the afternoon of December 22, Bayard, flushed and breathless from the lung ailment which he had contracted in St. Petersburg and which would soon claim his life, set out in search of Adams and found him on his usual stroll in the streets of Ghent. The British, Bayard gasped, had accepted the proposition.

The following noon the commissioners gathered for the last time to cavil over details and to iron out the last misunderstandings. By three o'clock they had finished their work, each agreeing to strike off three copies of the treaty. On Christmas Eve, as the bells of Ghent's cathedrals welcomed the holy day, three Englishmen and five Americans signed their names to the second Anglo-American peace treaty.

"This day," Adams wrote Louisa, "I consider the happiest of my life; because it is the day in which I had my share in

The signing of the Treaty of Ghent in 1814 marked the end of hostilities between England and the United States.

restoring the peace of the world." A few days later he added a more sober and rounded view of the treaty:

"We have obtained nothing but peace and have made great sacrifices to obtain it. But our honor remains unsullied; our territory remains entire. . . . It has left open not only all the controversies which had produced the war; but others not less important which have arisen from the war itself. The treaty would more properly be called an armistice than a peace, and the day we agreed to sign it I told my colleagues that it would immortalize the negotiators on both sides as a masterpiece of diplomacy, by the address with which it avoided the adjustment of any one dispute that had ever existed between the parties. Certain it is, that no other peace could be made."

And with characteristic honesty he acknowledged that Gallatin had "contributed the largest and most important share to the conclusion of the peace."

Great festivities celebrated the peace at Ghent. For more than two weeks both commissions were honored and toasted at balls and banquets and concerts where again and again the bands alternated "God Save the King" and "Hail Columbia." "I left this place," said Adams on his way to Paris, "with such recollections as I never carried from any other spot in Europe."

He had already written Louisa to close their establishment in St. Petersburg and to join him in Paris. On February 8, 1815, President Madison appointed John Quincy Adams "Envoy Extraordinary and Minister Plenipotentiary of the United States of America at the Court of His Royal Highness, the Prince Regent of the United Kingdom of Great Britain and Ireland."

This time there would be no confusion about his title.

7

A Successful Mission
to England

AFTER A THIRTY-YEAR ABSENCE, John Quincy returned to Paris to await the arrival of his wife and son before boarding the Channel packet for London, little suspecting that he would soon witness one of the most dramatic events of the nineteenth century. As he walked through the streets, the public walks and the squares, he found them "swarming with multitudes of human beings" just as they had been in April 1778 when he and his father had first driven up to their hotel on the Rue de Richelieu. "My imagination," he wrote, "can scarcely realize the fact that of the inhabitants of the city certainly not one in a hundred, probably not one in a thousand is the same. . . ."

Once again, as in his youth, he could not resist the lure of the theater and the opera. The Louvre Museum, which Napoleon had filled with the masterpieces of Europe as trophies of his conquests, was another great attraction. General Lafayette drove twenty miles from his country estate to visit Adams. John Quincy dined with the Count de Tracy and the Countess de l'Aubepin, and was presented to Louis XVIII and the royal family, including the Count d'Artois and the Duke and Duchess of Angoulême. As other monarchs had done before, Louis le Desiré inquired whether he was not related to "the celebrated Mr. Adams." In the midst of this tranquil scene a thunderclap was heard in the south.

"The Congress of Vienna," Adams wrote satirically, "had previously by solemn treaty constituted Napoleon Bonaparte Emperor on the island of Elba. On the first of March [1815], Louis le Desiré was quietly seated on his throne in the twentieth year of his reign by divine right, and in the first year by the bayonets of the allied armies. The Emperor of Elba lands in France with eleven hundred men and four pieces of cannon. On the twentieth day after his landing he takes possession of the palace of the Tuileries, after a triumphant and unresisted march of two hundred leagues. Louis le Desiré, who had proclaimed the Emperor of Elba a traitor and a rebel, and commanded him to be shot without a trial, escapes only by rapid flight beyond the French territory from being a prisoner. The Duke of Bourbon capitulates for permission to escape from the Vendée, the Duchess of Angoulême from Bordeaux, and the Duke of Angoulême, after attempting resistance a few days, becomes actually the Emperor of Elba's prisoner, and obtains only from his clemency the permission to quit the country. . . ."

Adams had followed the bulletins of Napoleon's return from Elba with incredulity and excitement: the unopposed landing at Cannes; the troops who refused to fire upon their Emperor and flocked to his standard; the capitulation of Grenoble; the unopposed entry into Lyons; and then the triumphant entry into Paris "amidst acclamations from the same multitude which has been for the last fortnight making the atmosphere ring with the cries of *"Vive le Roi!"* Up went the proclamations of Napoleon, *Empereur des Français,* pasted in fact over the royal notices ordering his arrest. "Between ten and eleven o'clock last night I saw in the garden of the Palais Royal," John Quincy wrote his father, "a huge bonfire of all the proclamations, indignations, execrations, verses and appeals to the people against the Corsican monster and tyrant, which had been loading the columns of the arches

The people of France cheered Napoleon's return from Elba.

the previous fortnight, and many of which had been stuck up there the same morning, probably by the same hands which were now with shouts of thunder committing them to the flames . . ."

John Quincy never met the emperor but he saw him from a distance several times. "I was present," he wrote his mother, "the only evening he attended at the Theâtre Français. . . . The House was so crowded that the very musicians of the orchestra were obliged to give up their seats, and retire to perform their symphonies behind the scenes. And never at any public theatre did I witness such marks of public veneration, and such bursts of enthusiasm for any crowned head, as that evening exhibited for Napoleon. . . ."

For Louisa Catherine and little Charles the emperor's return was a more painful personal experience. After an exhausting forty-day trip across Europe, they had crossed the frontier into France as Napoleon was taking possession of the Tuileries. Bonapartist troops marching south to join their emperor noticed the Russian make of Mrs. Adams's carriage. A great shout went up to drag out and kill the occupants. Fortunately an officer intervened to save their lives, keeping mother and son in custody until the troops had passed. From then on, she cried "Vive Napoléon!" every time a group of soldiers passed. That cry became her passport to Paris.

Adams believed that the resurgent sympathy for Napoleon came from millions of people who felt the farms and property they had gained in the revolution threatened by the Bourbon restoration. "The ancient nobility," he explained, "were asserting anew their claims to the feudal rights which had been so oppressive upon the people, and the priesthood, equally favored by the King and court were already clamorous for the re-establishment of tythes. . . . In the space of two months," he estimated, "the government of Louis XVIII has rendered itself more odious to the mass of the nation, than all the despotism and tyranny of Napoleon had made him in ten years." He would not predict whether the luck of the Corsican would hold in the new holocaust that was rapidly approaching. The Adamses were safely in London when the famous One Hundred Days came crashing to an end on a blood-drenched battlefield in Flanders.

Wellington's triumph at Waterloo reinforced Adams's customary penchant toward pessimism. The old balance of power between France and England, which the United States had exploited, was gone, and Great Britain was again the "dictatress of Europe." John Quincy wrote his father that wherever British influence reached, it was "busy blackening us in every possible manner." Great Britain found a receptive audience among the royalists everywhere who "despise us as Republicans." "Emperors, kings, priests, all the privileged orders . . . eye us with the most rancorous hatred. Among the crowned heads the only friend we had was the Emperor Alexander, and his friendship has, I am afraid, been more than cooled. . . ."

Fortunately, Great Britain's hostility toward the United States was moderated by the severe economic and social crisis which gripped the British Isles in the wake of the war. Furthermore, the foreign minister, Lord Castlereagh, had now become a firm advocate of Anglo-American reconciliation. Under the circumstances, Adams's mission to England, concerned primarily with settling the unresolved disputes of Ghent, was distinguished by substantial if modest diplomatic achievements.

Together with Gallatin and Clay, he negotiated a new commercial arrangement with Great Britain. If the agreement did not cover the knotty problems of freedom of the seas and American trade with the British West Indian and Canadian colonies, it did provide for the prohibition of discriminatory duties in the commerce between the two countries. This provision became a model for future trade pacts between the United States and other countries, and it is still in effect between the United States and Great Britain.

Acting on the advice of Secretary of State Monroe, Adams

proposed an agreement for the limitation of naval armaments on the Great Lakes. At first Castlereagh hesitated, but he finally relented when it became clear to him that unlimited armament was far more advantageous to the United States than to Great Britain. Referred to Washington for final disposition, differences were resolved in the celebrated Rush-Bagot Convention of April 28, 1817, which reduced the size and number of ships to the requirements of customs regulations. Initiating the great unguarded Canadian-American frontier, the treaty was viewed by Adams as a counterweight to Great Britain's uncontested mastery of the seas.

Real if less formal progress was recorded on the matter of the fisheries, which had been a source of discord in the American delegation at Ghent. John Adams maintained an unrelenting pressure on his son on this point, urging him to resign rather than "surrender one tittle or iota of the Treaty of 1783, relative to the fisheries." In one of his rare displays of temper toward his father, John Quincy bridled at the older man's unreasoning persistence. Such strictures should rather be addressed to New England, for only its determination to defend its own interests could buttress the position of the American ambassador. In a vehement letter to his father he commented that if "New England is as ready to resign [these rights] . . . as she was to resign her own children to the Helot-servitude of the press-gang you may rely upon it, they are gone. . . ." Nevertheless, John Quincy did not relax in his efforts, and he convinced the British foreign office to prolong from year to year its suspension of the ban on American fishermen and finally to refer the matter to Washington for settlement between the British ambassador and the Secretary of State.

On the once explosive issue of impressment, no agreement was in sight. This practice, however, fell into disuse as its economic cause began to disappear. Great Britain had initially resorted to impressment to save her supply of maritime labor, which during the war had been attracted to American ships because wages were higher than on British vessels. The end of the war threw thousands of British seamen out of employment, and hungry sailors were now demanding the exclusion of foreigners from British ships. Impressment had thus ceased to be a real issue between the two countries, but Adams was besieged by countless American sailors discharged from the press-gangs who sought passage home.

On instructions from Washington, Adams requested the return of slaves captured by the British during the war. He was greatly embarrassed when the British minister replying to his argument that Great Britain had violated its pledge by failing to return property seized in the war, took the humane position that a Negro was "a living and human being entitled to other considerations" than a table or a chair or other forms of private property. The issue was finally referred to arbitration, with Adams hardly suspecting that he would one day embrace the position of the Englishman as the great cause of his life.

Life in London was a pleasant relief for the Adamses after the cold winters in St. Petersburg. In comparison, they found even the climate "with its plague of waters" a "paradise." Louisa rented a small country house at Ealing, some eight miles from London, which was called Boston House. Their two older boys, George and John, were at long last reunited with the family and sent off to school. John Quincy hiked with them across the pleasant countryside; he encouraged them to master the art of fencing, taught them the use of firearms, and at night instructed them in the heavenly constellations. He was proud to see them hold their own in the unfriendly atmosphere of an English boys' school. One day George had been taunted by a schoolmate who, in an obvious reference to the British capture of the American capitol, asked him whether he had ever been in Washington. "No," proudly replied young Adams, "but I have been in New Orleans" (referring to the drubbing Jackson had given the English).

Once again, as at St. Petersburg, there was the round of court functions, the endless festivities of British aristocratic society: the queen's evening party, the prince regent's ball, a dinner by the lord mayor of London with the Austrian archdukes, and another with the Duke of Kent and Duke of Suffolk, a water party on the Thames with the Duke of Wellington. Once again Adams groaned at the inadequate salary of an American diplomat, which made it impossible to return these invitations, and again he wrote Monroe that "the permanent missions abroad must be exclusively given to men of large fortune willing to spend it liberally, or there must be a considerable increase of the salaries."

One of the duties of the ambassador was to minister to the needs, complaints, entreaties and proposals of all manner of persons, Americans and others who knocked on the door of the embassy or filled its mailbag with correspondence. There were inventors and "geniuses" who believed the minister of a republic would appreciate their talents and provide them with patronage. "One comes in search of suspected inheritance, and another of a conjectural genealogy. . . . An English father entreats me to find his son, a sailor who he hears entered the American service . . . and the friends of a beautiful young lady in America ask my permission to hunt up her father in England." And the last straw was an English lady who insisted that she be supported by the embassy because she had a husband in America. When Adams politely refused, she demanded that Adams intercede with the British government to collect the wages of her son, an American, who had fought on the side of the British in the battle of Lake Champlain! Adams prided himself in his general rule of being accessible to all persons, but he cried out "at the multitudes of people, who in person or writing apply for what cannot be granted, and often for what is improper, are so importunate, so improper, so unreasonable, sometimes so insolent and consume so much time. . . ."

The time they consumed was precious to the ambassador,

who with only a skeleton staff not only carried on "official business with the British government and reported to his own government, but remained in correspondence with the ministers, agents or consuls of the United States in Russia, Sweden, Holland, France, Spain, Italy, the Barbary Coast and Brazil, with the commanders of the American squadron in the Mediterranean, and particularly with the American consuls in the ports of Great Britain, Ireland, Gibraltar and Malta; and with the bankers and navy agents of 'the United States in the Mediterranean, at London, and at Amsterdam. . . ." And this was long before the age of the typewriter, teletype, telephone and telegraph.

The two years in London, full of hard work but generally happy, came to a fitting climax when James Monroe, recently elected President, invited Adams to become his Secretary of State. Besides Adams's superb qualifications and experience, Monroe wanted him as a New England man who would make the cabinet more representative of the nation as a whole, and because Adams's long absence from the country had kept him free from the blemishes and hatreds of partisan politics. Looking ahead, Monroe may have speculated that Adams would make an ideal successor to the Presidency, for which the post in the Department of State was then considered a stepping stone.

Old John Adams was overjoyed at the news. He longed to see his grandchildren again, and he could hardly contain his excitement at the prospects opening before his son. He urged John Quincy to accept without hesitation. "You are now approaching fifty years of age. In my opinion, you must return to your country, or renounce it forever. I am well aware of the critical situation you will be in. I know you have not the command of your feelings, nor the immutable taciturnity of Franklin or Washington. But you must risque all."

8

Ambassador Adams Is Appointed Secretary of State

John Adams's apprehensions were decidedly premature. It was not until later when John Quincy stepped out of the realm of diplomacy into the slippery arena of politics that the old man's premonitions would have the force of prophecy. Now John Quincy was at the peak of his diplomatic career. Minister to The Hague and to the Kingdom of Prussia, ambassador to the Court of St. James's and the Court of the Czar of the Russias, negotiator of the Treaty of Ghent, an eye witness of the turbulent era of the wars of the French Revolution and of Napoleon's rise and fall, he brought to the cabinet post a wealth of experience. He had a knowledge of the trends and personalities of world politics that no previous Secretary of State had possessed, and which would remain unequaled in the future history of the office. Recent biographers of John Quincy Adams ascribe to him many of the fundamental principles which served as the guidelines of American foreign policy in the century preceding the First World War.

John Quincy Adams's distinguished career as Secretary of State may also be attributed to two factors other than his experience. The first was a lull in sectional political differences during a period that has become known as "the era of good feeling." As New England turned its energies from commerce to manufacturing, the old disputes which had divided that section from the rest of the Union receded into the past. The Federalist party faded out of existence, and American politicians of the East, the South and the West cohabited peacefully in the great Republican coalition. Only the Missouri Compromise of 1819, which for the first time pitted slave states against free states, briefly upset the long era of tranquillity. Thomas Jefferson likened the issue to "a fire bell heard in the night." For John Quincy the dispute uncovered the "great and foul stain of slavery upon the American Union" whose "total abolition" might require the "temporary dissolution" of the Union and its "reorganization upon the principles of emancipation." A note from his diary of that time seemed to anticipate the third phase of his political career: "This object [abolition of slavery] is vast in its compass, aweful in the prospects, sublime and beautiful in its issue. A life devoted to it would be nobly spent or sacrificed." The questions raised in the debate over statehood for Missouri foreshadowed the fratricidal conflict, but for a time the problems seemed resolved.

The second factor that contributed to Adams's success as Secretary of State was his close working relationship with the President. A shift in the political scene may make allies of former enemies. Twenty years earlier Adams had denounced James Monroe, then ambassador to France, as a "Jacobin" and a member of the "French party" whose conduct subverted America's best interests. Now Adams remembered his vehement disapproval merely as "differences of opinion which time had mellowed." He viewed his role in Monroe's cabinet as that of a "subordinate" whose "duty" required him "to *support,* and not to counteract, or oppose, the President's administration. . . ." Who had changed, Adams or Monroe? Both—but mostly the world had changed and affected the old controversies. In any case, there was no recurrence of past disagreements, and Adams remained in his cabinet post through President Monroe's two terms of office.

The problems that faced Adams when he assumed office during the summer of 1817 were mostly a legacy of the War of 1812 and the still unfinished business of the Treaty of Ghent. Under Adams's patient supervision, Gallatin and Rush negotiated a new treaty with Great Britain which improved America's position on many of the old disputed issues. In other matters, among them England's territorial claims on the Maine frontier, Anglo-American rivalry on the northwestern coast and British interdiction of American trade with its colonies, Adams achieved no agreement, but his persistent efforts and his constant search for new openings and opportunities paved the way for future statesmen to settle, to America's advantage, most of these contended points. Adams's principal adversary, however, was not Britain but Spain, with whom the contest for possession of the Floridas was to become the burning, immediate problem of American foreign policy. Three months after his arrival at Washington, Adams became involved in this diplomatic bout, which extended over fourteen months and was finally crowned with a treaty that would exceed all expectations and constitute his great triumph as an American statesman.

With the exception of the distant Oregon wilderness still claimed by Britain, only Spain retained an empire in what is now the continental United States. The province of La Florida, East and West, remained in its possession, as did the emormous expanse of territory that began somewhere on an ill-defined western Louisiana border and extended westward through Texas as far north as the Rockies to the upper reaches of California and the Pacific Ocean. When negotiations began, American interest was focused almost exclusively on the Floridas. The Spanish colony of Florida was poorly fortified and in no position to resist invasion by any stronger power who might decide to use the territory as a base for new American conquest. It had become a menace to the security of the United States—thinking of its shape, Congressmen compared it to a pistol pointed at the heart of the country. The events leading up to the Florida crisis could be traced back to the earliest days of settlement in America.

The United States was only the last claimant for possession of the southern lands. Since the middle of the sixteenth century this vast territory had been coveted by the imperial powers of Europe. What the United States demanded as the fulfillment of its manifest destiny, Spain, France and England had claimed by divine right, reinforced by exploration and conquest, and surrendered only to superior force.

The conclusion of the American Revolution brought the United States and Spain face to face on the American continent. The two nations glowered at one another over a huge ill-defined frontier. Irritations, friction, and disputes among the settlers were frequent and led often to clashes. The pioneers wanted the Spanish-held lands for settlement and cultivation; the speculators wanted them for personal enrichment; the residents along the rivers patrolled by the Spaniards chafed at the regulations and restrictions placed upon their commerce. And Indian occupation of the borderlands, protected by Britain and Spain as a buffer territory, infuriated all groups. The Treaty of 1783 placed the American boundary on the eastern bank of the Mississippi and stipulated that the southwestern boundary should begin where the 31st parallel intersects the Mississippi. But Spain, refusing to respect the 31st parallel on the grounds that Britain's boundary of West Florida had been a hundred miles farther to the north, claimed the area to the Ohio and Tennessee rivers, and the Spanish flag flew over Natchez and other trading centers.

In the following decade the frontier crackled with incidents. The Spaniards shut down the Mississippi to American shipping. American adventurers promoted expeditions against Spanish territory. The Georgia legislature authorized land companies to sell acreage in a region held by Spain along the Yazoo and the Mississippi. Spanish river authorities confiscated contraband goods and arrested Americans. Indians gave sanctuary to runaway slaves in the Spanish domain; Americans violated the southern boundary, engaging in raids and skirmishes and settling on Spanish lands. Another European war was needed to bring peace, however temporary, to the troubled American frontier.

Defeated by the armies of revolutionary France and threatened by England, whose coalition she had deserted, Spain hastened to resolve its differences with the United States to avert an Anglo-American alliance against its American domain. In 1795, Thomas Pinckney, the American minister, wrung "from Spain's necessity" a settlement of issues that had been in litigation for a dozen years. In the Treaty of San Lorenzo, Spain conceded the boundary of the 31st parallel and granted free navigation on the Mississippi and the right of American citizens to deposit their goods in New Orleans pending transshipment and exportation. After two years of delaying tactics, Spain finally ratified the agreement. "You can't lock up an open field," was the comment of Foreign Minister Godoy, who had negotiated the agreement with Pinckney.

9

The Acquisition
of Florida

SECRETARY OF STATE ADAMS was no stranger to the Florida imbroglio. In distant St. Petersburg he had reflected on the martial summons of the war hawks to plant the American standard on the Gulf of Mexico as well as in the "frozen north." He had explored the meaning and consequences of Indian buffer zones over the conference boards of Ghent. The question in John Quincy's mind was not *whether* Spain would cede the Floridas but when and upon what terms. His chief concern was to conclude a fair settlement as quickly as possible.

His opposite number at the negotiating table was the Spanish minister to Washington, Don Luis de Onis. Skilled in the arts of diplomacy, devious in method, ingenious in his endless stratagems but always stubborn in purpose, Onis was a formidable if exasperating antagonist. "I have seen slippery diplomatists, more than one," Adams exploded in his diary, "but Onis is the first man I ever saw who made it a point to pass for more of a swindler than he was."

In a calmer moment, Adams's judgment would probably have been different, for Onis's diplomatic style was perfectly suited to the needs of the regime he represented—and that is the real measure of a diplomat. Spain was a sick, decadent world living off ancient glories that had long since receded into the past; its empire was dying and it was beset by revolution in the colonies and discontent at home. Restored to his throne by British bayonets, Ferdinand VII turned in blind fury on the liberals who had directed the valiant fight against Napoleon while he was in prison and imposed a vicious tyranny upon a suffering people. His foreign policy was a waiting game to delay the moment of reckoning as long as possible, a clutching at straws to save an empire whose dissolution was not only inevitable but imminent. Against all logic, he hoped that England would rescue his Florida estate, that the Holy Alliance would intervene against the revolutions in South America. Onis translated these chimeras into diplomatic terms, but he grew increasingly uneasy as he observed the growing sympathy in Washington for the revolutionary regimes on the southern continent.

On October 28, 1817, Adams noted in his diary, a representative of the "Government of Buenos Ayres" called upon him to present his own credentials as well as a commission from the "Government of Chile, signed by Director O'Higgins" to purchase "warlike stores." The next day the cabinet met to discuss the knotty problem of recognition. A month later Adams noted another fact, undoubtedly also remarked by Onis, to the effect that "Mr. Clay has already mounted his great South American horse . . . he intends to bring forward a motion [in Congress] to acknowledge the Government of Buenos Ayres, and perhaps Chile. . . ."

Lacking specific instructions from his government, Onis could do little more than continue the diplomatic dialogue with Adams, intrigue with the French ambassador, and stall for time. But a more dramatic event later that month set the alarm bells ringing in the foreign office at Madrid. The Spaniards had been overwhelmed on Amelia Island on Florida's east coast by a Scottish adventurer, Gregor McGregor, who took possession in the name of the republics of New Granada, Mexico and Rio de la Plata. He was soon supplanted by a more dubious French character, who had previously seized Galveston as a Venezuelan patriot and now converted the island into a haven for buccaneers and the slave traffic. Privateers under revolutionary flags sallied forth to attack Spanish shipping, and corsairs flying the flags of piracy raided the commerce of all nations. It was more than Washington could tolerate. On December 23, under President Monroe's instructions, an American naval squadron entered the area, sailed up the Amelia River and took possession of the fort in the name of the United States.

Fearing that if Spain delayed negotiations any longer it would lose the Floridas by seizure, the Spanish Foreign Minister Pizarro, hastened to dispatch Onis to the bargaining table. Onis had previously proposed to cede the Floridas if the Americans would accept the Mississippi as its western boundary line. Now he shifted the western border to a line drawn between the Mermentau and the Calcasieu rivers, in the middle of the present state of Louisiana. This maneuver was designed to create a barrier of distance between Spain's tottering Mexican province and the United States. Onis justified his map making on the grounds that the Louisiana Purchase had no validity because Napoleon had not kept his pledge to Ferdinand at the time of the retrocession and therefore had never held legal title to the territory. There was a grain of truth to the argument, and it had disturbed the consciences of many Americans at the time of the purchase. But Adams had not been one of them, and now, a firm believer in America's manifest destiny, he would not be deflected by disputes about the merits of dynastic property transactions. He countered the Spanish offer with the proposal to establish the Colorado River (of Texas) as the western boundary, from the Gulf of Mexico to its source "and thence to the northern limits of Louisiana."

The argument continued in a voluminous exchange of notes, but neither side retreated from its fixed positions. Onis wrote: "Truth is of all times and reason and justice are

founded on immutable principles. It is on these principles
that the rights of the Crown of Spain are founded in the
territories eastward and westward of Louisiana." Adams replied: "The observation that truth is of all times and that
reason and justice are founded upon immutable principles
has never been contested by the United States; but neither
truth, reason, nor justice consists in stubbornness of assertion,
nor in the multiplied repetition of error."

A stalemate had been reached which one historian described in these words: "Mr. Adams still stood upon the Colorado River of Texas; Don Luis was firmly planted between
the rivers Mermentau and Calcasieu. Between them lay half
the state of Louisiana and half the province of Texas." At
this point, Pizarro prevailed upon the British to intercede as
mediators. The British were willing but Adams and Monroe
were not, and the parleys came to a standstill.

Meanwhile the frontier was ablaze again, as the land mines
of social conflict planted in the Floridas during the War of
1812 began to explode. A British agent, Colonel Nicholls,
had organized and armed the Seminoles, exploiting their re-
sentment of Andrew Jackson's treaty establishing a defensive
and offensive alliance with the Creeks. Before leaving Florida
at the end of the war, Nicholls turned over to his Negro allies
a fort, well-stocked with ammunition, on the Apalachicola
River, close to the American border. It was known as the
Negro Fort because it was manned primarily by freemen and
ex-slaves; its leader, Garson or Garcia, invited the thousand or
more runaway salves in Florida to settle under the protection
of its guns, and Negro settlements sprang up for fifty miles
along the banks of the river. The community has been described by a Southern historian as the "only independent
Negro state ever attempted within the present United States."
Its existence filled the Georgia planters with alarm.

Jackson demanded that the Spanish governor suppress the
fort, and then, upon receiving an evasive reply, ordered its
destruction "regardless of its location in Spanish territory

and the Negroes returned to their rightful owners." The fort and all but a few of its three hundred defenders were blown to bits by a detachment under General Gaines, but the Negroes in the surrounding country escaped to King Bowlegs's villages on the Suwannee, a haven for fugitive slaves. So long as this refuge in East Florida existed, the human property of Southern slaveowners would not be safe, and they clamored for action.

The occasion was provided by clashes between Georgia frontiersmen and Seminoles, in which a number of scalps were taken by each side. Gaines was ordered to march against the Seminoles with instructions to pursue them, if necessary, across the Spanish border "unless they should shelter under a Spanish post." A few months later, the command and instructions were transferred to Andrew Jackson. On February 1, 1818, Old Hickory set forth, to the cheers of the Nashville population, on a campaign that would make diplomatic rather than military history.

It was a tattered and half-starved army that Jackson led through the wet wilderness into Florida. Most of the Indian braves had scattered before his advance. The few successful skirmishes that were fought resulted in the capture of several Seminole villages, which were burned to the ground, and the seizure of their stocks of cattle and corn. Another expedition plunged into an untracked jungle in an attempt to surprise the refugee Negroes in Bowlegs's villages, 107 miles away. But the Negroes were gone when they arrived. Instead of terminating his campaign, Jackson marched on the town of St. Marks, which, according to a rumor, was now in the possession of armed Seminoles. Contrary to his specific instructions, he invested the Spanish town but found no Seminoles. His only prisoner was an elderly Scottish gentleman, the Indian trader Arbuthnot, soon to be joined by Lieutenant Ambrister, an English soldier of fortune who had been captured in Bowlegs's country. Still on Spanish soil, Jackson arraigned the two English prisoners before an American court martial. They were charged and convicted of a variety of crimes, among them that of inciting the Indians to wage war against the United States. Arbuthnot was hanged and Ambrister was shot by a firing squad.

Now Jackson marched on Pensacola, the last lap of his sensational military junket. On the pretext that the Spanish governor, Masot, had conspired with the Seminoles, he stormed the fortress, which surrendered after a token resistance. The general appointed one of his subordinates military governor, declared in force the revenue laws of the United States, and then packed his bags and went home to Tennessee, amidst the wild applause of the American public.

President Monroe and his colleagues did not join the cheering. Andrew Jackson may have covered himself with glory, but he had precipitated the administration into an international crisis of the first magnitude. The very least of the consequences could be the disruption of the Florida talks. The British public was in an uproar: No foreign general had ever before executed British subjects with impunity, and they considered the grounds for execution flimsy. Angry speeches in parliament demanded a declaration of war. From Pizarro in Madrid came a blistering note protesting "the sanguinary executions on Spanish soil of the subjects of powers in amity with the King," and he branded Jackson's pursuit of the savages beyond the Spanish Florida line as a "shameful invasion of His Majesty's territory." In Congress, Henry Clay denounced the executions as barbaric and proposed a motion to censure the frontier commander.

Between July 15 and July 21, 1818, the cabinet met five times to consider the crisis. At first all, with the exception of Adams, were of the opinion that Jackson, having acted entirely on his own responsibility without instructions either from the President or from Secretary of War Calhoun, should be censured or at least discharged. But Adams contended that the cabinet could not in all conscience repudiate the erring general, for if he was not beyond reproach neither were they.

Calhoun had not been ignorant of Jackson's previous unauthorized seizure of Pensacola when he entrusted the Seminole campaign to him. President Monroe had received a confidential communication from the general in the field urging the seizure of East Florida, and although he had not replied to the letter, he also had not revoked Jackson's commission. It was not unreasonable for the general to have assumed that if he won the President would accept political responsibility for the victory.

Furthermore, Adams argued, the diplomatic consequences were of cardinal importance. As a show of force, he held, Jackson's undisciplined actions might conceivably strengthen America's hand in the Florida negotiations, while a repudiation of the general could be construed as a sign of weakness. This was not the only time in American history when a cabinet would be troubled by a headstrong military leader. After long debate, a compromise was reached. The note drafted by the Secretary of State on the President's instructions disclaimed responsibility for the seizure of Pensacola and St. Marks, but it refused to censure the general; it also declared that Pensacola and St. Marks would be returned as soon as a Spanish force adequate for defense against the Indians was prepared to take possession.

What effect would the American stand have on Great Britain? Pizarro awaited the English reaction before deciding his final course. He also pinned some hopes on the effects of the possible passage of Clay's resolution denouncing Jackson, which was then pending before Congress. In the interim, the Spanish minister made two tentative moves. First he broke off all further discussions with George W. Erving, the American ambassador at Madrid, until Jackson should be censured and the possessions he had seized restored to Spain; this demand was expounded in a lengthy diplomatic note. Then he secretly instructed Onis to continue exploratory discussions with Adams and to make further boundary concessions on the western border.

It was in these discussions that Adams unfolded his full vision of the westward expansion of the United States. He was prepared to retreat from the Colorado to the Sabine River. (This had been Monroe's suggestion, although neither he nor Adams was aware at the time of Onis's secret instructions providing, if necessary, for the concession of the Colorado River line. Years later, Southern Congressmen would accuse Adams of sacrificing Texas by his forfeit of the Colorado River boundary.) But, Adams went on, the United States was equally concerned with its northern border, and he made the following proposal: The Sabine River from the Gulf of Mexico to 32° north latitude, then due north to the Red River, thence up the Red River to its source "touching chain of the Snow [Sangre de Cristo] Mountains in 37 25 n.l., 106 15 w.l., and following the chain of mountains north of 41; thence along that parallel of latitude to the South Sea [The Pacific Ocean]." This area roughly included all of the present-day western United States with the exception of part of New Mexico, Arizona, Utah, Nevada, California and part of Colorado. Today this area may seem small to us; in Adams's time it was a veritable empire.

This proposal marked the final stage of the exploratory talks. When Onis, continuing his delaying tactics, countered with a slightly revised version of his original proposal, Monroe decided the moment had come for more resolute measures. He directed his Secretary of State to withdraw all previous boundary offers, reserving all claims to the Rio Grande River from the Gulf of Mexico to its source as the southwestern boundary of the Louisiana Purchase. The ultimatum was designed for domestic as well as diplomatic purposes. Monroe needed a quick victory in the Floridas to silence the irrepressible Henry Clay, whose campaign in Congress against Jackson was intended in part to discredit the administration and to further his own ambitions for the Presidency.

At about this time, Pizarro's note to Erving arrived in Washington, and it presented the perfect foil for the counter-attack against Clay. Adams drafted a vigorous riposte to Pizarro in the form of a letter to Erving intended to be made public. It was his most brilliant state paper. First he took upon himself the vindication of Jackson, who, he wrote, had been actuated by "motives of . . . purest patriotism . . . acting in the first law of nature—self-defense." The Spanish government, he declared, had proved itself incapable of defending its provinces, and he warned in a resounding peroration that the United States "can as little compound with impotence as with perfidy." The accusation of "perfidy" was a thinly veiled thrust at Great Britain and its agents in Florida, whose activities had already been roundly indicted in the letter. The document was, in fact, as much a challenge to Britain as an arraignment of Spain. In more recent times, historians have criticized Adams for his unqualified defense of Jackson; but whatever the weaknesses of some of his arguments they do not detract from the vigor of this philippic. Jefferson found it "among the ablest compositions" he had ever seen, "both as to the logic and the style," and suggested that it be circulated and publicized in Europe as an illustration of the level of American statecraft.

Copies of the letter quickly made their way to the European chancelleries, particularly to the British foreign office, where it had a telling effect. Lord Castlereagh called off the war dogs; he was prepared to sacrifice the cause of Arbuthnot and Ambrister—and all of Florida that the United States wanted—for the sake of a peace policy that would keep open the North American market for British manufactures. In Congress, the opposition led by Henry Clay was thoroughly deflated. Adams had successfully defended Jackson against Clay, but the future would see a strange reversal of roles in which Adams, supported by Clay, would battle for his political life against the attacks of Jackson.

The Secretary of State had crushed Pizarro's two principal hopes—British intervention and Clay's opposition. Spain was anxious now to cut its losses in the north so it could regain its

empire in the south, to free its hands of Monroe and Adams
for the combat with the South American liberators, Bolívar
and San Martín. In the second week of 1819, the two statesmen resumed their discussion, and for the next five weeks an
entire continent was the range of their negotiations. At the
last moment, Onis posed a final demand before he would
sign a treaty. He insisted that the midchannel of the Sabine,
the Red and the Arkansas rivers, not the southern and
western banks, as Adams had proposed, be the boundary line.
At an informal reception, Monroe, in a moment of fatigue,
yielded the point to Onis. But Adams was uncompromising,
and he carried the point to the cabinet, where Monroe de-
sisted in his favor. "You are harder to deal with than the
President," Onis told the Secretary of State.

On February 22, 1819, the anniversary of Washington's
birthday, the two men signed the treaty, which was virtually
identical with the version first proposed by the Secretary of
State. It was a momentous occasion for Adams and for the
nation. "It was perhaps the most important day in my life,"
he wrote in his journal late that night. "The acquisition of
the Floridas has long been an object of earnest desire to this
country. The acknowledgment of a definite line of boundary
to the South Seas forms a great epoch in our history. The
first proposal of it in this negotiation was my own. . . . It was
not even among our claims in the Treaty of Independence
with Great Britain. It was not even among our pretensions
under the purchase of Louisiana—for that gave us only the
range of the Mississippi and its waters. . . ." He might have
added that America's destiny had also been promoted, however unwittingly, by the French emperor, who had under-
mined the Spanish empire, and by South American liberators,
from whom the empire had received the *coup de grâce*.

Adam's exhilaration was soon to be dampened by another
round of Spanish intrigue and procrastination. At the last
moment he had innocently agreed to a clause in the treaty
recognizing royal land grants made in the Floridas before the

signing of the treaty. Only when it was too late was he to discover that two days earlier Ferdinand had conferred virtually all of the land on three court favorites. There was little to be done now but to protest to Madrid, where the monarch, once again, as in the case of the Louisiana Purchase and Pinckney's treaty, withheld his signature for two long years. Finally, constrained by an internal revolution and a vote in the reconstituted Cortes, he ratified the treaty on October 24, 1820. The new treaty nullified the land grants that had put the taste of ashes in Adams's victory. The treaty was resubmitted to the Senate, which advised and consented on February 19, 1821.

10

Campaigning for President

THE ACQUISITION of Florida was painted on the broader canvas of the thrust for freedom in South America. The stirring exploits of Bolívar and San Martín had fired the imagination of Americans. In the popular mind, their deeds were a continuation of the struggle for independence which the thirteen colonies had begun in 1776. The people expected that their government in Washington, filled with the same generous impulse, would quickly recognize the infant South American republics and would surround them with friendship and, if possible, with protection from foreign intrusion.

But governments, even those born in revolutions, are usually motivated less by idealism than by considerations of statecraft and the national interest. The Secretary of State was circumspect in his reaction to the first demands for recognition of the newly created states. As an Anglo-Saxon Puritan, Adams doubted that a people so long subjected to despotic and clerical rule were capable of self-government. "They will be independent," he acknowledged, "but will they be free?" Furthermore, there was a danger that American recognition of South American independence might jeopardize the acquisition of the Floridas, and Adams had assured the Spaniards that his government would not act "precipitately" in this regard. America's self-interest, he held, took precedence over all other considerations.

The ratification of the Florida treaty, however, prepared the way for a change of policy. It did not come a day too soon. A rising tide of public opinion, stimulated by Clay's bombastic oratory in Congress, jolted the administration out of its cautious neutrality. With its blessing, Congress voted a resolution expressing their "deep interest . . . for the success of the Spanish provinces of South America which are struggling to establish their liberty and independence" and pledging to support the President "whenever he may deem it expedient to recognize the sovereignty and independence of the said provinces." As the policy changed and the United States became the first government to recognize the sovereignty of the new Latin nations, Adams's opinions also altered. In instructions to the American minister to Colombia, he hailed "the emancipation of the South American continent [for invoking] all that is precious in hope and all that is desirable in existence to the countless millions of our fellow creatures, which in the progressive revolutions of time this hemisphere is destined to rear and maintain."

New commitments brought new responsibilities. Hardly had the fledgling South American states declared their independence than they were menaced by the Holy Alliance, the coalition of "despotism and monkery," as Adams called it. The sword and shield of monarchical government, the Alliance had put down republican revolutions in many parts of Europe. Now the French, acting under the aegis of the Holy Alliance, marched into Spain to rescue Ferdinand from an uprising of democrats, and it was feared they might also try to recapture Spain's South American empire. A new conference of the confederated monarchs had been called to give France a legal fiat for its counter-revolutionary mission.

As it turned out, America's chief concern in defining a policy was Great Britain's attitude, rather than the more remote threats of the Holy Alliance. The disintegration of the Spanish empire had opened to Great Britain a vast new market for her manufactures. In competing for the good will of the revolted colonies, she had marked advantages. Her mastery of the seas, for example, could frustrate any attempted invasion, a protection the United States was not able to provide. At first the British proposed a joint Anglo-American declaration guaranteeing the integrity of Spain's former colonies from conquest by a third party. Adams was interested in the idea, but he instructed the American ambassador to inform the British that the precondition of a joint declaration was Great Britain's recognition of the independence of the Latin American nations. Unprepared for such a step, Lord Canning decided upon the unilateral course of extorting from the French government a secret commitment not to invade Latin America.

The administration in Washington was unaware of this secret compact when it was confronted with a new Russian note intimating that if the United States abandoned its neutrality, the czar, as the leader of the Holy Alliance, would support the aims of France and Spain in the new world, i.e., "the supremacy of Spain over its revolted colonies." The cabinet agreed that the time for action had come. Adams urged his colleagues to take an independent stand against the Holy Alliance, finding it "more candid as well as more dignified to avow our principles to Russia and France than to come in as a cock-boat in the wake of the British man-of-war." Out of the discussion which ensued was born the Monroe Doctrine.

The principal feature of this now historic statement of American foreign policy was the coupling of a warning with a pledge: a warning that interference of European powers in the western hemisphere would be considered an unfriendly act, and a pledge that the United States would abstain from any involvement in the affairs, alliances and wars of Europe. Adams was primarily responsible for this aspect of the declaration. He had strenuously objected when Monroe, inspired by ex-President Madison, had proposed to condemn the French intervention in Spain and to support the rebellious Greeks, and Monroe finally withdrew this proposal. Adams was being consistent with the tradition of United States foreign policy first enunciated in Washington's Farewell Address, continued by John Adams as second President of the United States, and only shortly before reiterated by the Secretary of State in a message to the czar directed through the American ambassador in St. Petersburg: "To stand in firm and cautious independence of all entanglement in the European system," he had declared, "has been a cardinal point of [United States] policy under every administration of their government from the peace of 1783 to this day. . . ." To those who felt that the United States should intervene when foreign causes were just, Adams had replied in his Fourth of July oration a year later: "America is the well wisher to the freedom and independence of all. She is the champion and vindicator only of her own." In Adams's opinion, crusades for freedom, in the Old World or in the New World, were not part of the mission of the United States.

In that same address, Adams had anticipated the non-colonization provision of the Monroe Doctrine. But while the doctrine had restricted its opposition to the reestablishment of colonialism in countries which had already attained their independence, Adams attacked the institution itself. "Great colonial establishments," he declaimed, "are incompatible with the character of our institutions. . . . They are engines of wrong, and in the progress of social improvement it will be the duty of the human race to abolish them, as they are now endeavoring to abolish the slave trade." In projecting the end of imperialism, Adams was far in advance of his century, but it should be added that he saw this as a desirable if distant goal rather than as an immediate objective of American foreign policy.

If Adams attached less importance to his role in forming the Monroe Doctrine than has been accorded by histori-

ans of later generations, it was because his preoccupation
with diplomacy was lessening as his thoughts and ambitions
turned toward the Presidency.

Nothing was more normal than John Quincy Adams's ambition to be President. At a tender age, he had already been
destined by his mother for a post "in the cabinet or in the
field," and his father thought him endowed with the qualities of "genius." Together they had watched with great care
over his career, guiding, counseling, alternating praise with
admonition and criticism. If ever a man's family had been a
school for the Presidency, it was John Quincy Adams's. His
abilities were recognized by Washington, Madison and Monroe, who had assigned him to important diplomatic posts.
Under ordinary circumstances, Adams would have been expected to move naturally and with little friction or opposition from the Department of State to the White House, just
as Madison and Monroe had done before him.

But these were not ordinary circumstances. America was
now in the throes of great change, greater than the change
which accompanied the Jeffersonian upheaval at the turn of
the century. Monroe's second inauguration in 1820 marked
the end of the long "era of good feeling." The tranquil, unhurried America of small farmers and tradesmen, aristocratic
planters and merchant princes clustered in the narrow space
between the Atlantic seaboard and the Alleghenies was passing into history. Population had increased to 6,000,000, almost double that of the Revolutionary era. Even more
important was its distribution. In 1790 the inhabitants of the
trans-Allegheny states numbered a little over 100,000, while
there were 1,000,000 in New England. But by 1830, the population of the Western states had jumped to more than
3,500,000, nearly 1,500,000 of which were located north
of the Ohio River, while the population of New England
was slightly less than 2,000,000. Eleven new states had been
added to the original thirteen. Four cities had more than
40,000 inhabitants each, and two had more than 100,000.

Four revolutions were proceeding almost simultaneously,

marking each section of the country with distinct economic characteristics. In the East, the industrial revolution was replacing commerce with manufacture and household crafts with factories, shifting the centers of economic activity from the harbors to the waterfalls and bringing into being a new class of factory workers. In the middle states, a transportation revolution was changing life and occupation. The Erie Canal and Fulton's steamboat joined the East to the West. Other canals linked the waterways, and a network of turnpikes spread out in every direction from the big cities. With the new markets thus opened in the West, banks, insurance companies, turnpike and canal and steamboat companies multiplied. The population of New York City, the terminus of this trade, jumped from 123,000 in 1820 to 202,000 in the next decade. In the West there was a land revolution. Settlement and real estate speculation had increased purchases of land from the government from 1,000,000 acres a year in 1815 to five times that number in 1819, resulting in an economic crisis and the first angry cries against the Eastern "money power." In the South, the cotton gin had revolutionized agriculture, bringing with it the cotton-slavery economy and shifting the area under cultivation from the spent lands of the tidewater region to the cheaper and more fertile areas of the Gulf and the West. As the tidelands declined, the sun set upon Virginia's ancient aristocracy and brought to an end the long reign of the Virginia dynasty in Washington.

No section was as yet powerful enough to claim the succession alone, and no issue had yet arisen to create a genuine division. The issues of slavery, tariff and internal improvements were still only in their nascent stage, and the tendency toward compromise was much stronger than that toward conflict. Under these conditions, the hopes, aspirations and differing interests of the sections found expression in men rather than in issues. In consequence, the 1824 campaign became the first popularity contest in the history of the Presidency.

One can hardly imagine a more unlikely winner in such a

contest than John Quincy Adams. He was anything but a popular man—and he knew it. To those who criticized his utter lack of the kind of charm and the back-slapping conviviality that are the hallmark of the politician's trade, he replied with a disarming if melancholy candor: "I am a man of reserved, cold and forbidding manners; my political adversaries say, a gloomy misanthropist, and my personal enemies, an unsocial savage. With a knowledge of the actual defect in my character, I have not the pliability to reform it."

An even more serious drawback than the lack of an ardent personal following was the absence of a political machine to publicize his name, effect alliances, and wage an aggressive campaign. The support of New England, which preferred even Adams to the proslavery candidates, might have been the basis for such a machine. But Adams would not encourage a partisan organization in his behalf. He stood upon a record of public service and professional integrity. "If the people wish me to be President," he said, "I shall not refuse the office; but I ask nothing from any man." He told a distinguished Philadelphia Congressman, who urged the formation of a campaign organization, that he would not "take one step to advance or promote pretensions to the Presidency." With typical self-righteousness, he wrote in his diary that "if that office is to be the prize of cabal and intrigue, of purchasing newspapers, bribing by appointments, or bargaining for foreign missions, I have no ticket in that lottery." But Adams did have a ticket, and as no other prize was dearer to him, he was eventually to play the game according to its rules.

Opposing Adams was a galaxy of popular, personable and influential men, who were not encumbered by the scruples and conscience that handicapped the New Englander. Two were members with Adams of Monroe's cabinet. William Crawford, Secretary of the Treasury, was at the outset the leading contender in the field. Virginian by birth and resident of Georgia, he commanded the support of the South, and he augmented his following by freely bestowing upon

DeWitt Clinton

John C. Calhoun

Andrew Jackson

William Crawford

Henry Clay

Opposing John Quincy Adams in the 1824 presidential campaign were a galaxy of popular, personable, and influential men. CULVER PICTURES, INC.

friends the favors of office. John C. Calhoun, Secretary of War, also a Southerner, hoped at first to supplant his colleague for his section's allegiance but decided early in the campaign to postpone his larger ambitions and content himself with the Vice-Presidency, which he won virtually without competition. The popular DeWitt Clinton, former governor of New York, also withdrew before the final stage of the campaign. The West was represented by two outstanding political figures, Henry Clay and Andrew Jackson, although the influential Speaker of the House was soon outdistanced in the race for the loyalties of his region by the hero of New Orleans.

Jackson was also John Quincy Adams's preference. Had he not himself been a candidate, he would certainly have thrown his weight on the side of the frontier general. Adams had quarreled with Clay at Ghent and had suffered his opposition in Congress during the Florida negotiations. He considered Crawford totally corrupt, "a worm preying upon the vitals of the Administration within its own body." Of his five opponents, Jackson alone in Adams's mind would administer the government with perfect integrity and disinterestedness. At the opening of the election year, Adams gave a great bail to celebrate the anniversary of the victory at New Orleans, with the general the honored guest. A thousand persons, all of fashionable society, were present at the gala event, and throughout the long evening of festivities Jackson reserved his gallant attentions for the Secretary of State and the charming hostess. How far it must have been from Adams's mind that evening that the man whom he so sincerely admired and whom he had once defended alone in the cabinet and against the whole world would soon become his most inveterate, irreconcilable enemy!

Popular interest was intense as the hard-fought campaign reached new heights of political activity and depths of abuse and calumny. Stump orators extolled the virtues of the candidates, pamphlets were published and circulated, resolutions were passed. On Mississippi steamboats, in stagecoaches and taverns and at military parades, Jackson's men canvassed for support. A session of the United States Circuit Court in Ohio was reconvened immediately after adjournment to constitute itself as a kind of a state nominating convention where judges, jurymen, attorneys, plaintiffs, defendants and witnesses from all parts of the state endorsed the candidacy of John Quincy Adams. In Philadelphia members of "Hickory Clubs" wore black silk vests stamped with portraits of Jackson. In Boston's Faneuil Hall, a great meeting acclaimed Adams as the popular choice, and the endorsement was echoed by all the state legislatures of New England. Maine paid tribute to his "splendid talents, incorruptible integrity, republican habits and principles."

Elsewhere Adams's candidacy was attacked as dangerous to Republican institutions, since it seemed to perpetuate a custom of the outgoing President choosing the Secretary of State as his successor. Jonathan Russell, raking up the dead leaves of Ghent, accused Adams of having betrayed the country to protect New England's fishery rights and advance his own personal fortunes. Jackson was denounced as the murderer of Arbuthnot and Ambrister; Clay was branded as a gambler and a drunkard; Crawford was accused of dereliction of duty and personal dishonesty. No praise was too extravagant, no calumny too base. Even Clay, a veteran of the rough-and-tumble of political warfare, complained of the "bitterness and violence of Presidential electioneering. . . ."

When the smoke of battle had cleared, Jackson emerged as the popular choice. In the voting for Presidential electors he had received 153,544 votes to Adams's 108,740, Clay's 47,136 and Crawford's 46,618. But in the electoral college the votes were divided as follows: Jackson, 99; Adams, 84; Crawford, 41; Clay, 37. Since Jackson had failed to receive a majority of votes in the electoral college, the election was thrown into the House of Representatives, where each of the twenty-four states would cast one vote, and a majority of thirteen was required to elect. The choice was among the three highest scorers in electoral votes, which eliminated Clay from the contest. In fact, only Adams and Jackson remained in the race, as Crawford had suffered a paralytic stroke and was no longer a contender.

Adams now confronted the great political dilemma of his career. He could acknowledge that Jackson was more representative of the popular will and step aside in his favor. Or he could play the lottery of a House election, where influence, promises, maneuvers and bargains would determine the winner. If ambition triumphed over conscience in the battle Adams fought within himself, it was because he had gone too far in the game to be able to retreat. Moreover, he saw nothing conclusive in the popular vote. In six of the states, electors had been chosen by the legislatures rather than at the ballot box. In one of these, New York, which had the largest population, Jackson had little popular following. Elsewhere property qualifications for voting made the electorate unrepresentative. The great democratic movement of factory workers, frontiersmen, small farmers and speculators that was building up for Jackson was not more than a trend in 1824, and Adams was not inclined to interpret a mere trend as an overwhelming expression of public opinion.

All eyes were now on Henry Clay, who was courted by the major contestants. In losing his bid for the Presidency, he had acquired the position of kingmaker. Jackson needed the three states in Clay's column to obtain a majority. For Adams the addition of Clay's states would still leave him lacking three votes, which could be obtained only by a shift from the Jackson or Crawford column. Clay inclined to Adams rather than Jackson as a matter of hard political calculation. His future would still be open if the New Englander won, while it was extremely unlikely that he could succeed another Westerner to the Presidency. A bargain with Adams was clearly indicated, provided Adams would agree.

As Clay's emissaries multiplied their approaches, Adams hesitated, but only momentarily. "I am treading on coals of fire," he told himself. Four of the states whose votes in Congress Clay controlled or could influence were Western states, unmistakably pro-Jackson. In the case of Kentucky, Clay's home state, the legislature had instructed its representatives to vote for Jackson in preference to Adams in the runoff. Illinois was represented by a lame-duck Congressman who aspired to the governorship of the territory of Arkansas. Louisiana's vote was also on the auction block. In addition, the vote of Maryland, divided between Adams and Jackson, might be obtained through an arrangement with Daniel Webster. Jackson's agents were also busily engaged in political trading, and only time would tell which trade conformed best to the opinions of the electorate. As the new year began, Clay accepted Adams's invitation to visit him at his home, and all that evening the two men surveyed the alignments in the approaching Congressional vote and discussed their own roles in the coming administration. An agreement was achieved which assured Adams's election, but had incalculable consequences on the political careers of both men.

Electoral maneuvers continued feverishly through the months of January and February. Adams now appeared assured of the votes of the six New England states, Maryland, Ohio, Kentucky, Illinois, Missouri and Louisiana. The only uncertainty was New York, whose legislature had previously given Adams twenty-six of its thirty-six votes. But the Congressional delegation was now evenly divided, seventeen on each side, between Adams and Crawford. One man alone was undecided, the wealthy patroon Stephen Van Rensselaer. Clay and Webster used all their persuasiveness to swing him into the Adams camp, but seemingly without success. That night, legend has it, forty-eight hours before the election, as the New York delegation balloted to decide its choice, Van Rensselaer bowed his head, praying for divine guidance. He opened his eyes to see on the floor a paper on which the name of Adams was written. Van Rensselaer picked up the message from heaven and dropped it in the ballot box.

On February 9, 1825, Congress elected John Quincy Adams

on the first ballot. He had received the votes of thirteen
states to Jackson's seven and Crawford's four. This was the
second Congressional runoff for the Presidency: in the first
John Adams had been defeated for a second term. The old
patriot glowed with happiness upon learning that his first-
born had followed in his footsteps to the position that Abigail
had called "the guardian of his country's laws and liberties."
With trembling hand he wrote: "The multitude of my
thoughts and the intensity of my feelings are too much for a
mind like mine, in its ninetieth year."

For John Quincy Adams there were more somber moments. He had hoped to be the unambiguous choice of all
the people. He was in fact a minority President, representing
one section of the country, and the choice of a coalition of
politicians. With typical honesty, he replied to the committee headed by Daniel Webster, which officially notified him
of his election, that a more conclusive popular verdict would
have been desirable. He was aware that one of his worthy
opponents had received a larger number of "primary electoral suffrages" than he, but the failure of either of them to
win an absolute majority had made necessary the runoff in
the House of Representatives. He would decline the office if
the means were available to resubmit the election to the
people in order to arrive at greater unanimity. As this was
not possible under the Constitution, he had no choice but
to accept "the post assigned to me by the call of my country,
signified through her constitutional organs. . . ."

The President-elect was aware, too, that a successor was
already waiting in the wings, with a large following impatient for him to take command. At Monroe's reception on
election night, it was Jackson, the defeated candidate, and
not the new President who attracted the public's curiosity
and admiration. The general was the essence of cordiality
itself, and at the inauguration a month later he stepped forth
to shake Adams's hand. This was the last friendly gesture, for
already Jackson's allies were whetting the axes of vengeance.

11

A Second Adams in the White House

At ELEVEN-THIRTY on the morning of March 4, 1825, John Quincy Adams took his place in the horse-drawn carriage that waited before his home on F Street. Headed by an imposing escort of militia, resplendent in their parade dress, and followed by a cavalcade of citizens, the procession moved on to the Capitol to inaugurate the sixth President of the United States and the second Adams to fill that post. For two sleepless nights, John Quincy had pondered over his dubious victory. He had not been elevated to the highest office as "the man of all the people," as he had so devoutly hoped in the first flush of his political ambitions. He had been frustrated in that aim by a host of political enemies who had alienated the sympathies of a substantial portion of the people. Perhaps, he reflected, they had merely won a battle but not the war, and from the Presidency itself, a position of commanding influence, he might yet unite the nation around his person. This thought provided the keynote of the Inaugural Address.

With a masterly hand he traced the prodigious growth of the nation. Since the ratification of the Constitution, its boundaries had been extended from sea to sea, its population had quadrupled, and the number of states had increased twofold; "the forest has fallen by the ax of our woodsmen; the soil has been made to teem with the tillage of our farmers; our commerce has whitened every ocean." The dissensions over theories of government and foreign policy aroused by the wars of the French Revolution had now abated. "Ten years of peace, at home and abroad, have assuaged the animosities of political contention and blended into harmony the most discordant elements of political opinion." There were, to be sure, great dangers of discord in sectional and occupational differences, but, he exhorted, if the citizens would make "one effort of magnanimity" and discard the remnants of rancor against one another, the Union might be knitted together on a truly federal and national basis. He closed with an earnest entreaty to Congress and the people: His heart and his faculties were all in the service of the task, but as a minority President he needed above all their indulgence. The future of the Adams administration depended on whether this plea would be heeded.

It was in this conciliatory mood that Adams began to construct his cabinet. Attempting to bridge the gulf between the factions, he offered the post of Secretary of War to Jackson, and the Treasury post to Gallatin if Crawford refused to keep it. When the three men declined, he nominated Richard Rush of Pennsylvania as Secretary of the Treasury and James Barbour, former governor of Virginia, as Secretary of War; both were Crawford supporters. John McLean of Ohio, a follower of Calhoun, was continued as Postmaster General, and William Wirt remained as Attorney General. New England, to which Adams principally owed his election, remained unrepresented. The most controversial nomination, of course, was that of Henry Clay as Secretary of State. To Adams, Clay was a most natural choice. His qualifications were beyond question, and his presence in the cabinet gave the West, in Adams's opinion, an important place in the top councils of the nation. To the opposition, it was crowning proof that Clay was being rewarded for the "corrupt bargain" with Adams that had won him the Presidency. For four years, this would be the strident battle cry of Jackson's multiplying army of supporters.

The ambitious Calhoun thought he had uncovered the fatal weakness of the Adams administration that would permit him to manipulate it as Hamilton had attempted to manipulate John Adams's administration. Through an emissary, the South Carolinian brazenly threatened to take the South into Jackson's camp unless Adams set aside his own choices for the cabinet and appointed the men Calhoun insolently designated. With a few well-chosen words, Adams sent the emissary flying and red-eared back to his arrogant master.

From the West, where large gatherings were acclaiming Jackson on his return to The Hermitage, the frontier general exploded with indignation. "So you see," he wrote his campaign manager, "the Judas of the West [Clay] has closed the contract and will receive the thirty pieces of silver. His end will be the same." Like a winged message, his words flew through the back country, and soon the epithet "Judas of the West" was heard on all sides. In Tennessee, the legislature accepted Jackson's resignation from the Senate and at once renominated him for the Presidency. The campaign of 1828 had already begun, only a few days after Adams had taken occupancy of the White House, and with all the rancor he had so desperately tried to avoid.

If the prospects seemed unpromising, Adams continued to believe that the way to overcome the opposition was not to stoop to their level in a mud-slinging contest, but to attempt to unite the people behind a great national objective. Through the summer and autumn of 1825, he examined and sifted the problems and needs of the people, weighed the means for their solution, and consulted with his cabinet colleagues on how the program should best be introduced to Congress. Adams had put the finishing touches on his first State of the Union message when the legislators convened in Washington that December.

Its principal theme was the overriding need of the nation for "internal improvements," which today are called public works. The great object of civil government, Adams declared, was to improve the condition of its constituents. As the country expanded and settlement penetrated into distant regions, and as agriculture and manufacturing developed, roads and canals were indispensable to transport men and produce from region to region and to link together the city with the countryside. It was a thought which he had already expressed in the reference in his inaugural address to "the roads and aqueducts of Rome [which] have been the admiration of all after ages and have survived thousands of years after all her conquests have been swallowed up." But the obligation of government encompassed moral, political and intellectual as well as physical improvement. Its efforts should be devoted to the advancement of learning and science. For this he proposed research to achieve a uniform standard of weights and measures, the establishment of a national university, and the building and equipping of an astronomical observatory with provisions to finance an astronomer and publish his findings. "It is with no feeling of pride as an American," Adams argued, "that on the comparatively small territorial surface of Europe there are existing upward of one hundred and thirty of these light-houses of the skies, while throughout the whole of the United States there is not one. . . ."

He did not urge Congress to exceed its powers in legislating for "the improvement of agriculture, commerce and the manufactures, the cultivation of the mechanic and of the elegant arts, the advancement of literature, and the progress of the sciences, ornamental and profound . . ." but he warned them of the danger of neglect. "While foreign nations," he challenged, "less blessed with that freedom which is power than ourselves are advancing with gigantic strides in the career of public improvement, were we to slumber in indolence or fold up our arms and proclaim to the world that we are palsied by the will of our constituents, would it not be to cast away the bounties of Providence, and doom ourselves to perpetual inferiority?"

The program that Adams advanced with great trepidation seems almost commonplace in our times, when the government not only builds highways, housing, schools and dams, insures the unemployed and the aged, and engages in meteorological, oceanographic and chemical research, but invests billions of dollars in projects for the uses of nuclear energy, sends astronauts whirling into outer space, and plans expeditions to the moon. Yet Adams's modest proposals were received with consternation, denounced in thundering tirades as the rankest heresy and as the consummation of a plot begun by his father to impose a monarchy upon the United States. Men laughed, and they jeered and derided the "lighthouses of the skies" as they had once, ages past, hooted at the idea that the world was round.

Adams and his colleagues were thoroughly stupefied. To one degree or another, all the candidates in the last election had favored internal improvement—at least none of them had opposed it. For Eastern, Middle Atlantic and Western states, public works were an economic necessity and the means, so it had seemed to Adams, to unite them politically around his administration. He had not reckoned with the South. As the slave system in that region had become very profitable, it had also become more vulnerable, and its defenders became increasingly sensitive to Northern agitation. Only recently the legislatures of six Northern states had adopted resolutions calling for the manumission of the adult children of slaves and their recolonization in Africa. Then had come Adams's public works plan, which clearly widened the powers of the federal government at the expense of the states. For the South this constituted an implicit threat against slavery, the survival of which required an impotent federal government and a strict enforcement of the doctrine of state's rights. For the next thirty-five years the interests of the country as a whole would take second place to the profits and privileges of the slaveholding aristocracy.

Meanwhile the cry went up in Virginia that Adams was reaching out for the powers of a Caesar. The aging Jefferson emerged from his retirement to shake a warning finger against the renewal of Federalist longing for "a single and splendid government of the aristocracy. . . ." In the West, Jackson's campaign managers skillfully exploited the apprehensions of the settlers, who feared that internal improvements would be financed by an increase in the price of public lands, increasing their dependence on speculators and Eastern banks.

The next great opposition bugbear was the apparently innocent issue of the Panama Congress. Bolívar had summoned the South American states to a conference at the Isthmus of Panama to join their defenses against foreign intervention as the first step in the political unification of the southern continent. The congress would also discuss a plan for the liberation of Cuba and Puerto Rico from Spanish rule, the suppression of the slave trade and the recognition of the independence of the Republic of Haiti. It seemed only natural that the United States, which had so warmly proclaimed in the Monroe Doctrine its sympathy for its neighbor republics to the south, should participate in the Congress. The first champion in the United States of Latin American independence, Secretary of State Clay, responded enthusiastically. But the diplomatic Adams presented a more moderate proposal to Congress. The American mission, he informed them, would be instructed to abstain from joining any league of states, but it would seek an agreement for freedom of the seas and a treaty of commerce reciprocally favorable to all the participants; it would also seek religious freedom in these exclusively Catholic countries. On the other hand it would neither extend recognition to Haiti, nor approve the contemplated plan of Mexico and Colombia to expel the Spanish imperialists from Cuba and Puerto Rico. Despite these reservations, Adams endorsed the Panama Congress, whose design he said, "is great, benevolent, humane. It looks to the melioration of the condition of man. . . . It is congenial with the spirit which prompted our declaration of independence."

Anticipating every possible objection, Adams could hardly have been more conciliatory. But the opposition, now led by Martin Van Buren, an astute Northern politician, feared that participation in the projected Congress would redound to the political advantage of the Adams administration and revive its waning prestige. The cause of South America had always been popular with the American public, and any measure to foster the liberty of the new republics against the universally despised Holy Alliance was bound to meet with warm and generous approval. As a result, Van Buren calculated, the public would visualize the alliance of Adams and Clay not as a "corrupt bargain" but as an association for great and noble works. Hence it was decided to pull out all the stops, to play upon every fear and prejudice and misconception in a frontal attack against the Panama mission.

Adams was assailed for wanting to involve the country in entangling foreign alliances, for deserting the principles of Washington's Farewell Address, for courting war with the Holy Alliance. But the big guns were fired by the Southern Congressmen who swore that the government would never have their consent to enter into a league with states which had abolished slavery, wanted stern measures for the suppression of the slave trade, demanded the recognition of the Negro Republic of Haiti, and sought to free Cuba and Puerto Rico and emancipate their slaves. Never would they consent to invoking the Monroe Doctrine on behalf of such republics.

"Slavery," declared Haynes of South Carolina, "must ever be treated as a domestic question. . . . With nothing connected with slavery can we consent to treat with other nations. . . . These governments have proclaimed the principle

of equality and liberty. They have marched to victory under
the banner of universal emancipation. You find men of color
at the head of their armies, in their legislative halls and in
their executive departments. Our policy with regard to
Hayti is plain. . . . Let our government direct all our ministers in South America and Mexico to protest the independence of Hayti; but let us not go into council on the slave
trade and Hayti. . . ."

Berrien of Georgia devoted his attention to Cuba and
Puerto Rico, whose disposition, he declared, must have serious consequence on that portion of the United States where
slavery existed. Their liberation, he continued, by "a people
whose fundamental maxim it is that he who would tolerate
slavery is unfit to be free, that the principle of universal
emancipation must march in the van of the invading force,"
would be the signal for slave insurrections in the South.
"What then is our policy?" he clamored. "Cuba and Puerto
Rico must remain as they are. To Europe the President has
distinctly said we cannot allow a transfer of Cuba to any
other European power. We must hold a language equally
decisive to the South American states."

The finishing touches were provided in a fierce diatribe by
John Randolph of Virginia. Randolph was notorious for his
eccentricity, but he was a master of invective, with a power
of phrasemaking and sarcasm that cut like a rapier. He appeared in Congress in a riding habit and cracked his whip
against his boots to emphasize his savage thrusts. As he spoke,
a little Negro boy provided him with porter to quench his
thirst. "I have borne some humble part," he cried, "in putting down the dynasty of John the First [John Adams], and
by the Grace of God, I hope to aid in putting down the dynasty of John the Second." He raked over the dead embers
of the father's role in the Alien and Sedition Acts and
cracked his whip as he charged the son with having deserted
the Federalist Party to foster his own career.

The full fury of his raging rhetoric he reserved for a cli-

matic assault upon the association of Adams and Clay. This
he compared with "the coalition of Blifil and Black George
—the combination unheard of until then, of the Puritan with
the blackleg." (Blifil and Black George are two characters in
Fielding's novel *Tom Jones*; Blifil is a hypocrite and Black
George a scoundrelly gamekeeper.)

Clay challenged Randolph to a duel, and the two men exchanged pistol shots in a meadow on the right bank of the
Potomac. But the only damage was to Randolph's cloak. The
debate on the Panama mission dragged on until late April
1826, when both houses approved the Presidential recommendation, but the congress had adjourned when the American representative finally arrived. The opposition had
accomplished its purpose. It had tarnished the image of Pan-
American collaboration as an asset of the Adams administration; and the "Blifil–Black George" coalition became a
byword throughout the nation. Few men at the time noted
that from their high ground of moral righteousness the opposition had stooped to the most immoral of combinations.
Although Adams had been their target, the real victim was
the principles of freedom their fathers had fought for in 1776,
which were now to be denied to the Caribbean nations to protect American slaveholders and to advance their own political
fortunes.

Adams took no public notice of Randolph but described
him in his diary as "the image of a great man stamped on
base metal" who in "speeches of ten hours long . . . drunk
with bottled porter, and in raving balderdash . . . reviled
the absent and the present, the living and the dead." He
trained his fire against Calhoun, who, as presiding officer of
the Senate, had failed to call Randolph to order and thus had
been remiss in his duties of preserving the decorum of debate and an attitude of respect between the branches of the
government. His trenchant indictment of Calhoun was published under the *nom de plume* Patrick Henry in *The National Journal*. Calhoun, writing as Onslow, replied in the

National Intelligencer that as he was not a member of the Senate he had no power to call a Senator to order. Unique in American history, the pamphlet war between President and Vice-President continued for some time. Public opinion was aroused on Adams's side, and in its next session the Senate amended its rules, empowering the Vice-President to preserve the amenities of orderly parliamentary debate. John Randolph was demoted by the Virginia legislature from the Senate to the House of Representatives as a punishment, so Adams preferred to believe, for his "outrageous" conduct.

A truce fell over the political battles that summer when the nation learned that John Adams, aged ninety-one, had died. On the bright, sunny morning of July 4, 1826, the fiftieth anniversary of independence, the old Patriot had awakened for the last time. "It is a great day. It is a good day," he said of the fete he had already commemorated in a toast addressed to his townsmen with the words: "Independence Forever!" That afternoon, as he drew his last breath, he whispered almost inaudibly: "Thomas Jefferson survives." Seven hundred miles away, Jefferson lay on his deathbed at Monticello, and at almost the same hour, asking, "Is it the Fourth?" he joined Adams in the last journey. As the bells tolled their dirge, men spoke in hushed tones of this remarkable coincidence. "Two of the principal actors," to use John Quincy's words, in America's freedom, "the hand that penned the ever-memorable declaration and the voice that sustained it in debate," had been stilled on the fiftieth anniversary of that proclamation. In that half century the two men had been united in friendship by common purpose, divided by seemingly unbridgeable political differences, and then reconciled in retirement, maintaining a regular correspondence which since has become famous in American letters. "Such men need no trophies, they ask no splendid mausolea. We are their monuments; their mausoleum is their country, and her growing prosperity the amaranthine wreath that Time shall place over their dust." So read the Adjutant General's Order of the Day to the Army.

Too late to attend the last rites, the President journeyed back to Quincy to pay his final respects to the man who had been father, counselor, educator and political mentor and whose temperament and career so strongly resembled his own. Waves of "inexpressibly painful" emotion welled up in John Quincy as he walked through the old house and entered his father's bedchamber, where he had exchanged opinions with the old man on his two last summer visits. Everything was the same, except in the terrible feeling of loneliness at the absence of his parents; the charm had vanished—"the charm which has always made this house to me an abode of enchantment." Contemplating his bleak political future, Adams thought that in two or three years he would retire and return to his father's home, where he had spent the happiest days of his life. It would be a safe and pleasant retreat to pursue his literary inclinations, if only, like his father, he could sustain the solitude of total retirement after an active and agitated life.

Adams remained in Quincy amidst the memories of his boyhood days in the Revolution until the New England landscape brightened with the flood of colors of the changing autumn foliage. In October he was back at his desk in Washington to resume his duties. Throughout the day, visitors, official and unofficial, invited and uninvited, crowded into his office. Heads of departments and other government officials sought advice and instructions. Foreign diplomats called to pay their respects. And then came the hordes of office-seekers, citizens with a plan or a complaint, politicians and inventors, men and women seeking pardons for relatives and friends or subsidies for themselves. The doors of the White House were wide open in those days; there were no secret service corps, security checks, or screening. People just walked in and waited their turn. A government official, dismissed for misconduct, threatened the President's life unless he found him a new position. Adams was not intimidated, but he saw the man again and again. Sometimes he bridled at this "nest of spiders." At other times he smiled at the persistence of the solicitors, as in the case of the pretty woman requesting a position for her husband. "There is no pleader of this cause," he chuckled in his diary, "so eloquent as a young and handsome woman and none who ought to be more firmly resisted."

When the "spiders" had gone, the heavy chore of paper-work began: messages to Congress, communications with other departments, the transcribing of documents, political and personal correspondence. On into night he worked by the light of kerosene lamp and with no help except from his son John, who was the President's private secretary and his entire secretarial staff.

Adams rose at five or six every morning. In the winter months it was before dawn when he started his daily four-mile hike, usually returning home in time, he said, to see the sun rise from the eastern chamber of the Presidential mansion. Sometimes he varied the procedure by joining his son John in a canter on horseback around the capital. Swim-ming was his favorite sport and means of relaxation. He prided himself in being able at the age of sixty to swim a mile across the Potomac in one hour. Every day at sunrise, on sultry Washington summer mornings, he would go down to the river, strip to the skin, and plunge in for his daily swim. His one other diversion was botany, particularly the domestication of wild trees and shrubs, and he husbanded a variety of exotic plants on the White House grounds.

The midterm elections of 1826 decided the fate of the administration. There were now majorities hostile to the President in both chambers of Congress. The opposition's first action was to replace the pro-Adams Speaker of the House, whose antislavery stand in the Missouri crisis had aroused the enmity of the South, with a Virginia man, the kind of disreputable type, Adams said, who always rise to the top in "troublous times." The opposition had won be-cause it had consolidated Jackson's Western following with the Southern forces of Calhoun and Crawford and the powerful political machine directed by Van Buren in New York. A new party was hacking its way through the political scene with the same inexhaustible energy with which the frontier settlers, who were its backbone, blazed their trails through the wilderness.

Adam's defeat in the midterm elections had another significant cause: He had stubbornly refused to use the time-honored means of building a network of political supporters. He would not reward his friends and punish his enemies. Government service, in his unshakable view, was an office of public trust to be awarded only to the competent and the qualified and to be terminated only in the absence of such qualities or for unimpeachably good cause.

Thurlow Weed had been chiefly responsible for swinging New York into the Adams column in 1824, thus assuring his election. Weed traveled to Washington to persuade the President that General Tallmadge, the public leader of the Adams party in New York and onetime spokesman of the antislavery forces in the House, was entitled to a distinguished appointment. Weed departed empty-handed for Albany and never returned to Washington. His case was typical. Old friends of Adams's, influential in New York or Pennsylvania politics, were turned away, their entreaties ignored or refused. In a bitter letter, one former enthusiastic worker for the Adams cause complained to the President that the effect of his attitude would be to drive his friends into private life, obliging them either to conceal their political preferences or retire entirely from the political arena. Another, even more outspoken, said there was not one kind personal feeling for Adams among his friends.

More dangerous yet were the political enemies Adams permitted to retain key government positions. They were a Trojan horse within the administration. A man named Sterrett, the naval officer at New Orleans, consistently abused the administration, reviled the President, and publicly organized against the Louisiana Congressmen who had voted for

Adams. There were other such men among the collectors of customs in the various ports. But the most notorious of all was John McLean, the Postmaster General, who was a close friend of Calhoun's and a determined foe of the administration. McLean used his position to discriminate against supporters of Adams and appoint supporters of Jackson and Calhoun to positions in his department throughout the country. There was little question of his duplicity and treachery, but in the absence of overt proof Adams refused to remove him because he was an able official and had made the postal service more efficient than it had ever been. If he accepted the principle of punishing political opponents, Adams repeated time and again to his worried and aggrieved supporters, the public service would be at the mercy of a political inquisition which would undermine its purpose and effectiveness and make slander rather than competence the key to appointment. "Such a system," Adams wrote a friend, "would be repugnant to every feeling of my soul."

The result of Adams's honorable conduct was to discourage his friends and disorganize the forces working for his reelection while the opposition was lodged like termites within his administration. Even so, the opposition did not hesitate to attack his integrity. In the reconvened Congress they accused the President of operating a vast system of patronage. Resolutions were introduced for Constitutional amendments to prohibit the appointment of Congressmen to public office; demands were made that the President report on appointments made during his term. Where facts were lacking, reference to the Clay "bargain" was usually sufficient to bolster the innuendo of general corruption. In fact, little was done in the two final years of the Adams administration; Congress divided into two hostile camps and warred for the prize of the 1828 elections. Casting off all restraint in his personal reflections, Adams described his adversaries in Congress as "bitter as wormwood in their opposition . . . drunk with faction though not with alcohol," although some he said were "frequenters of gin lane and beer alley."

Like the debates in Congress, the Presidential campaign quickly degenerated to the level of character assassination. In pamphlets, newspapers, handbills and stump speeches, Adams was subjected to merciless abuse, a veritable rain of falsehood and half truth. He was accused of voting against the Louisiana Purchase, of ceding Texas to Spain, of trading Mississippi navigation for fishing privileges, of being both a Federalist and a renegade from Federalism. He was denounced for having spent public funds to purchase a billiard table and a chess set for the White House, objects he had paid for out of his own pocket. His detractors said that Adams, like his father, had been supported all his life by government funds as a public official and they cited the total salary he had received from 1809 to 1817.

But the opposition's most powerful weapon against the administration was the so-called "corrupt bargain" Adams had contracted with "the Judas of the West." Clay believed that this charge would finally be discredited when he discovered that an ambitious young Pennsylvania politician, James Buchanan, acting on his own responsibility, had approached Jackson before the last election with an offer of Western support if Clay was promised the Secretary of State appointment. Jackson, of course, had believed the offer had come from Clay, and that when he had refused to commit himself, Clay had sold his votes to Adams. Clay demanded that Buchanan publicly acknowledge his actions, and he assumed that the accusations would cease. But the scandal did not subside. Adams had no illusions, and he told Clay that once suspicion had become a popular delusion, truth would remain unheard until "the sacrifice" was "consummated." "General Jackson," he predicted, "will therefore be elected."

Adams's campaign spokesmen were no more punctilious with truth and fact, no more charitable than their opponents. Jackson was portrayed as a ruffian, a professional duelist and a murderer. He was accused of having been a confederate of Aaron Burr, of speculating in Florida lands while he was governor of the province, of murdering Ambrister and Arbuthnot, of having court-martialed and shot six mutinous militiamen at New Orleans. But the most cruel attacks cast aspersions on Jackson's marriage, which may well have hastened the death of Rachel Jackson and forever ended any hope of personal reconciliation between Adams and the general. In every way it was one of the most desperate, despicable campaigns in the annals of American politics.

These were not the issues, however, which decided the election of 1828. Mighty currents of social change were uprooting parties and institutions, social customs and political opinions. The Jacksonians rode the tides to victory while the Adams party was swept into oblivion. From four diverse factors—rapid manufacturing growth, vastly improved transportation facilities, westward expansion, and the South's reliance on agriculture for economic stability—there arose a great democratic ferment. Farmers, settlers, factory workers, the increasing mass of common people, insisted on political recognition, equality of opportunity, a greater share in the nation's wealth, the elimination of inequitable laws. They demanded an end to the domination of the favored few of New England and the southern tidewater regions over the government.

Radicals, plebeians, and populists worked tirelessly to do away with property qualifications for voting. They agitated for an end to the system of imprisonment for debt, which annually crowded the jails with 75,000 debtors, many of whom owed trifling sums. In New York and Philadelphia, journeymen mechanics were organizing the first labor unions to reduce the sunup-to-sunset working day. Workingmen's associations were clamoring for free education which would provide their children with opportunities hitherto open only to the wealthy. In the wake of these movements came a host of politicians impatiently awaiting the upheaval that would fling open the doors to government positions and political careers.

Jackson was the superb symbol for this movement. His

humble beginnings and his frontier upbringing marked him as a man of the people. He had risen to prominence, unlike all previous aspirants for the Presidency, without benefit of family fortune or university education. His quick temper and his rough and even uncouth manner were character traits now esteemed by the rising new democracy. In addition, his record as an Indian fighter and his triumph at New Orleans made him a popular hero. Against this model of popular virtues, Adams was hopelessly outclassed. Aloof and unapproachable, he lacked the common touch. His background—Harvard, New England Federalism, the diplomatic service, the very fact that he was an Adams!—were all handicaps in the eyes of a public that was suspicious of men of learning, distrustful of diplomats, and resentful of the first families of New England and everything associated with the old regime.

One other factor favored Jackson against Adams. Slavery was not an issue in the campaign, but it was already a force in American politics, and the security of its "peculiar institution" had become a criterion of political choice for the South. Faced with a choice between Jackson and Adams, the South preferred Jackson, a slaveholder who was distinguished by his ruthless pursuit of fugitive slaves in the Florida campaigns. Adams, despite his extreme caution, was identified with the rising antislavery sentiment of the North. The combination of Western and Middle Atlantic democracy with the slave South, effected by Jackson's managers, became the key to the opposition's triumph.

The results of the voting, as expected, were overwhelming. Jackson had won by a landslide with 647,276 votes to Adams's 508,604, gathering the electoral votes of all the states except the New England states, New Jersey, Delaware and Maryland, for a total of 178 to 83 for Adams.

Even Adams, who had long foreseen his own defeat, found the results a shattering political and personal repudiation. He was overcome by the blackest mood of depression. "The sun of my political life," he wrote in his diary, "sets in the deepest gloom." To friends who urged him to look ahead to the next election or to a seat in the Senate, he declared he had no other intention now than to withdraw from "public affairs" and to "go into the deepest retirement."

In the faltering light of his lamp in the overcast dawn of New Year's Day 1829, Adams brooded over the "ruins of his Administration" and his personal disaster. The Presidency, a realization of the hopes of a lifetime, had been the cruelest of disappointments. Instead of uniting the people in a truly national government as he had hoped to do, he had been faced with a coalition of popular forces determined to settle the scores of the controversial election of 1824. They had fulfilled Randolph's malediction in meting out to the son the same fate that had overtaken the father in the previous generation.

There is no mystery in the tragic denouement of the career of the two Adamses. Men of great integrity and high quali-fications, both were conservatives who took office in a ground-swell of radical change. As the light always burns brightest before it is extinguished, they had the illusion that they were traversing a passing crisis that would soon be overcome. Not until it was too late did they realize that they had been the last holdouts of a passing order, filling a brief interim in which popular forces would build up irresistible power for the assault on the citadels of conservatism. John Adams was overwhelmed by the Jeffersonian upheaval, John Quincy Adams by the Jacksonian revolution.

After his defeat, John Adams had retired from political life, and he spent the remaining years at his home in Massa-chusetts. In the bleak winter of 1829, John Quincy Adams anticipated a similar future.

12

Ex-President Adams Is Elected to Congress

JOHN QUINCY ADAMS's political misfortune was followed by a host of personal woes. He had left office in 1829 a relatively wealthy man. His savings would have been enough to assure a retirement free from financial worries (Presidents did not receive pensions in those days) had it not been for a disastrous investment he had made while Secretary of State. At that time, flour and grist mill properties owned by one of his wife's relatives were being threatened with foreclosure. John Quincy had invested heavily in the mills, expecting them to provide employment for his son John and a steady income for the family during his retirement. It was a bright hope which, like so many others, began to fade. The mills went from bad to worse. They were poorly managed by George Johnson, Louisa Adams's cousin. Bad crops, damage from storms, competition from the West, which was intensified by the opening of the Baltimore and Ohio Railroad, all conspired against a profitable business operation. During the winter of 1829 and 1830, young John was put in charge of the mills and managed, by strenuous work and unceasing devotion, to save the property from bankruptcy.

In the midst of financial problems the Adamses suffered the tragic loss of their eldest son. On the morning of April

30, 1829, George Washington Adams was reported missing on the *Benjamin Franklin,* as the steamboat, which the young man had boarded in Boston on the way to Washington, reached Long Island Sound. George was considered the most brilliant of the three Adams boys and was expected to be the heir to the Adams niche in history. He had been an outstanding student at Harvard, ranking first over Ralph Waldo Emerson in the competition for the Boylston Prize. He studied law in the offices of Daniel Webster, was admitted to the bar in 1824, and two years later was elected to the Massachusetts legislature. His brilliance veiled only too thinly an emotional instability which brought his promising career to an early end. It may have been that his family's expectations and the Puritan sternness of his upbringing weighed too heavily upon him. A sensitive young man, he was broken in the conflict between duty, which drove him into law and politics, and his natural inclination for poetry, drama and the arts. Constantly in ill health, he neglected and even mismanaged his father's financial affairs, with which he had been entrusted. His law practice declined, and soon, despite constant parental admonition—all too constant! —he began to go deeply in debt, each time begging for and receiving aid from his stern but forgiving father. He was at his lowest ebb when his father asked him to come to Washington. Full of self-reproach, his mind apparently gave under the strain, and strange images beckoned him to seek peace in the sea before the ship reached port.

His parents were crushed with grief. Their boy had been only twenty-eight years old, born in Berlin during Adams's first full diplomatic mission and named for the nation's first citizen, to whom Adams owed the appointment. John Quincy blamed himself for so persistently urging upon his son a life "foreign to his nature." Louisa Adams was inconsolable and soon became physically ill. For weeks John Quincy sat at her bedside comforting her and nursing her back to health. Because of her weakened condition she remained in Washington after her husband and son John left for Quincy to prepare the old mansion for occupancy. On the return voyage they read in a New York newspaper that George's body had drifted with the tide to City Island, where it had been found. Father and son journeyed to East Chester to attend funeral services. The coffin was later sent to Quincy for burial.

Less than five years later the Adamses' second son, John, died. After he had put the mills on a sounder basis, his health began to deteriorate, and in the following two years his illness became acute. Finally, at the urgings of his father, he left for Quincy in the hope of recuperating there, but it was too late. Summoned to Quincy, Adams arrived a few hours before his death. John, the least talented of the three sons, had long been his father's close friend and an efficient steward as well as his private secretary when President. John Quincy had lost more than a son. "A more honest soul, or more tender heart," he wrote, "never breathed on the face of this earth."

"John's Grave" was the title of Louisa's grief-stricken poem:

> Softly tread! For herein lies
> The young, the beautiful, the wise. . . .

The social climate which Adams found in his home state did nothing to alter his mood of despair. An ex-President, returning to his native community to live out his remaining years, is usually received with honors and warmth. This was the case in his home town, where the citizens of Quincy welcomed him and surrounded him with tokens of their affection. But Boston was frigid. A sullen animosity pervaded the leading Federalists of the State Street aristocracy.

They had been mortally offended by a reference Adams had made in the last months of his Presidency to the secessionist "Hartford conspiracy" during the days of the Jeffersonian embargo. The issue, at least a quarter of a century old, had been lost in the mists of history until Adams, drawn involuntarily into public dispute by a Southern opponent, contributed to its reappearance. After the election, the surviving New England Federalists of that period demanded a public explanation from Adams. As diplomatically and moderately as possible, Adams recapitulated the incontrovertible facts, now buttressed by new evidence. The right was clearly on Adams's side, and in subsequent years when nullification and states' rights became burning political issues, New Englanders would have occasion to regret the stillborn secessionist movement of their Federalist forebears. Meanwhile relations were hostile between Adams and men who had been the intimate friends of his youth. He was snubbed, almost ostracized, and, in a cutting gesture, dropped as president of the American Academy of Arts and Science, an honorary post which he had held for twelve years.

Slowly, painfully, the elder statesman began to settle down among the familiar scenes of his boyhood. The great old house he had inherited from John Adams had been sadly neglected. It was almost bereft of furniture and in bad need of repairs. The lands had been untended, and the garden and orchard had run to weeds. With his son Charles, who made frequent visits from Boston, John Quincy bent himself to the task of making the estate livable. He worked in the garden, planted and pruned in the orchard, arranged and classified his library, and tramped for miles through the marshes with his brother Thomas. In warm weather he plunged into the water for his daily swim off Daniel Greenleaf's wharf, and at the age of sixty-two he recorded that he could make the half mile down the creek to Quincy Bay and back in sixteen minutes flat.

Now, at long last, he began what was to have been the great literary endeavor of his retirement: the biography of John Adams. He also completed notes for a history of political parties in the United States. Meanwhile, Boston slowly thawed out and John Quincy Adams was again a welcome guest at the dinner tables of its leading citizens and at public

The house in Quincy, Massachusetts, in which John Adams and John Quincy Adams were born.

functions. An indication of the change was his election to the Board of Overseers of Harvard University. The most dramatic sign of this new approval, and one that would produce a metamorphosis in the life of John Quincy Adams, came in September 1830. It was the offer by prominent local citizens of the nomination for Congress from the Plymouth district, which now included the township of Quincy.

It was a highly unconventional proposal, especially for tradition-bound New England. There was no precedent for it. No past President had ever returned to political life by occupying an elective office in the national legislature. Washington, John Adams, Jefferson, Madison and Monroe had retired to their rural estates as distinguished elder statesmen, discreetly offering their advice and opinions on matters of state, delivering an occasional ceremonial address, and only rarely making a public pronouncement on a political issue. One might have expected that this pattern would have had almost the force of law with John Quincy Adams, whose political career to this point had been tailored on strictly conventional lines. Far from it! Not only did he see no wrong in it—there was nothing degrading, he said, in an ex-President serving the people as Representative in Congress or in any other elective office—and he also clearly implied to the committee that he would accept if chosen by a clear and unambiguous majority of the electorate. He had thrown his hat in the ring without hesitation.

The Adams family was appalled—and opposed. They had been subjected for thirty years to the ordeal of public life, an ordeal climaxed in strains, tensions, hatred, character assassination, and then the bitter disappointment of public rejection. Now they hoped at last for personal life, privacy, for a tranquil and leisurely old age. The most persistent opponent was young Charles, who had married into a prominent Boston family and was now starting out on his own career. Why, he demanded of his father, do you not devote yourself to your writing? Because, replied Adams, I must fulfill my destiny. Please leave destiny out of it, retorted the son. Very well, Adams agreed, destiny may be an ill-considered expression, but my decision is firm, and "I am prepared to take blame to myself for all the decisions that befall me."

In truth, Adams lacked the talent to make him an outstanding writer. Later generations in the Adams family would make their mark as historians, philosophers and sociologists. But John Quincy Adams was the supremely political animal. He was intensely interested, as one of the most learned Americans of his time, in history, science and religion, but politics provided the zest of his life. He thrived in the charged atmosphere of legislation, conflict and disputation. The smoke of political battle was like oxygen for the lungs of the old warrior. Without it he felt his life wasted, without purpose. There really was never the slightest doubt that John Quincy Adams would accept the nomination, nor the slightest possibility that anyone could alter his decision.

On November 1, 1830, Adams was elected to Congress, having received three-fourths of the votes cast, with two other candidates dividing the remainder between themselves. He was jubilant, even though, he wrote in his journal, "the dearest of my friends have no sympathy with my sensations. . . . No election or appointment conferred upon me ever gave me so much pleasure."

Thus, at the age of sixty-three, when most men are lost in thoughts of the past, John Quincy Adams was anticipating with the excitement of a young man his third political career. Out of it there would be born a dramatically new reputation as radically different from the previous one as though a new man had filled the skin of the old.

Adams was fully aware of the hazards and pitfalls that beset his new excursion into politics; introspective and inclined to pessimism, he probably exaggerated them. He was entering a Congress controlled by a party which had won its victory at his expense. In their eyes, Adams's highly unorthodox act was viewed as an attempt to refurbish his image in the public's mind as a prelude to another bid for the Presidency. In an unequal struggle against an unfriendly administration which held all the levers of power in its hands, Adams, as a solitary Congressman, could be thoroughly crushed and his reputation ruined, while people shrugged their shoulders at the quixotic old man who could not stay home and count his blessings. "How do you feel," Henry Clay teased him good-naturedly, "upon turning boy again and going into the House of Representatives?"

Yet the omens were not all unpromising. There were some three hundred callers at the Adams house in the capital on New Year's Day. The ex-President found much good will for him among legislators, diplomats, judges, and important public officials. His first committee appointment in the House was to the Committee on Manufactures. Because of his unfamiliarity with the complexities of such problems as the tariff, Adams demurred, but unsuccessfully, and he eventually became one of the most effective members of the committee, writing elaborate reports which served as the basis for legislation. From then on, during his long tenure in the legislature, Adams was always the most methodical, the best informed, and usually the hardest-working member of the various committees on which he served.

Among his most significant appointments was the chairmanship of a special House committee charged with the disposition of a legacy of $500,000 left the United States by an Englishman, James Smithson, "for the increase and diffusion of knowledge among men." This was the origin of our now famous Smithsonian Institution. Adams had always been passionately devoted to scientific advancement in the United States. As Secretary of State he had occupied his spare hours, often working late into the night, with the preparation of a voluminous study on the standardization of weights and measures. The building of a national astronomical observatory had been a favorite, albeit unsuccessful and politically costly, project of his Presidency.

To Adams the Englishman's bequest was like manna from heaven: Since the funds were at hand and required no special appropriation, there was no valid argument against the establishment of an educational or scientific institution. Even so, Calhoun and his followers denounced the project as an infringement of states' rights. In his report to Congress, later republished in an edition of 5,000 copies, Adams undertook to instruct the young nation in the benefits of learning and to dramatize the event as a landmark in the development of American culture. "The attainment of knowledge," he asserted, "is the high and exclusive attribute of man, among the numberless myriads of animated beings, inhabitants of the terrestrial globe. . . . To furnish the means of acquiring knowledge is therefore the greatest benefit that can be conferred upon mankind. It prolongs life and enlarges the sphere of existence. . . . To what higher and nobler object could this generous and splendid donation have been devoted?"

In the ten years that Smithson's legacy waited on the meanderings and delays of parliamentary debate, Adams never relaxed his vigilance, watching the funds with all the tenderness and ferocity of a lioness guarding her cubs. He pursued two aims with inflexible purpose: first, to establish and equip a national astronomical observatory; and second, to prevent any attempt to deplete the funds by random contributions to needy schools or colleges or by creating administrative sinecures for friends of the party in power. As a result of his watchdog tactics, the Smithson funds were kept intact through the years of indecision. The establishment of a "light-house of the sky" was a by-product of his untiring efforts. While Congress rejected his proposal for an observatory and designated that the bequest be used for a museum of scientific pursuits, Adams's many reports, constantly proselytizing for his idea, finally awakened wide public interest. This led to the building of a naval observatory, which was eventually renamed the National Observatory. Posterity would inscribe the name of John Quincy Adams alongside that of Benjamin Franklin as one of the nation's early patrons of science.

On the great issues which divided the nation during Andrew Jackson's second term, Adams, who had entered Congress without party attachments, was often, although not always, on the side of the man responsible for the most shattering defeat of his life. Although his personal antagonism to Jackson sometimes distorted Adams's judgments, it rarely influenced his actions.

As chairman of the Committee on Manufactures, Adams devised the tariff bill of 1832 and won its acceptance by Congress. It was a compromise measure, steering a middle course between the protectionists of the North and the free-traders of the South. It was also the kind of tariff the South had accepted many times in the past. This time, South Carolina, led by Calhoun, hoisted the standard of rebellion, declaring the federal tariff an encroachment on the rights of the states and therefore null and void in all the ports of South Carolina. This was the famous Nullification crisis, the dress rehearsal for secession and civil war some thirty years later.

Because of Jackson's affinities with the slave system, Adams expected him to retreat before the Southern threat. It was an incredulous Adams who watched and supported Jackson's vigorous measures, which routed the rebels of the Palmetto State. Guided by Constitutional principles, which Adams himself had enunciated before the crisis, Jackson had won the battle to preserve the Union. To Adams, however, it was a dubious victory, for if the nullifiers had been put down, Congress, under their bullying threats, had enacted a new tariff which conceded the substance of their demands. Adams believed that the slaveholders, with Jackson's aid, were fast becoming a "privileged class of citizens," to the detriment of the free-labor system of the manufacturing North. This theme of his first antislavery speech during a debate in the House was denounced by a South Carolina Congressman as "a firebrand thrown into the Hall." It was not he who had thrown it, Adams retorted: "The Nullification Ordinance is the firebrand."

In Jackson's long and uncompromising war against the Bank of the United States, Adams was clearly aligned with the conservatives. A close friend of Nicholas Biddle, the bank's president and a Hamiltonian by conviction, he was a staunch supporter of the sound-money and hard-credit policy which ranged the wealthy classes against homestead farmers, small entrepreneurs and Western speculators. Unmoved by their grievances, Adams was unalterably opposed to any measure which tampered with the currency or weakened the authority of the national bank as the indispensable guardian of the sanctity of private property. That it was a doomed and unpopular position did not for a moment inhibit John Quincy's convictions. In a speech intended for Congress and later reprinted as a pamphlet in a large edition by Nicholas Biddle, he predicted inflation and bankruptcy as the consequences of state-chartered banks. In this aspect of the problem his views were prophetic.

The same conservative philosophy led Adams to oppose the abolition of imprisonment for debt, an appalling law that permitted a citizen to be jailed for failing to pay the most paltry debt and then starved him in prison if he was unable to pay his board. In resisting this humanitarian reform, Adams, one of the most enlightened men of his time, took a stand that belonged in the dark ages. On the eve of his great crusade against chattel slavery, this medieval view of the supremacy of property rights over human rights is a shocking paradox in the career of John Quincy Adams.

There were no reservations, however, in Adams's support of Jackson's tenacious efforts to wrest a settlement of long-standing claims from the French government. They dated back to the Napoleonic Wars, when French privateers had freely raided and seized American shipping. Recurrent but unsuccessful attempts had been made to collect this claim under the Monroe and Adams administrations. But it was Jackson who finally succeeded in negotiating a treaty stipulating payment of some $5,000,000 from the French government. The treaty was signed by Louis-Philippe, but the French Chamber of Deputies refused to ratify it. Relations between the two nations rapidly deteriorated, and Jackson decided that after a twenty-five years' delay, the United States would act. Urging reprisals on French property, he requested from Congress the means for retaliation in case of emergency. Although there was danger of war, the Whig leaders in Congress, particularly Daniel Webster, viewed it not as a national crisis, but as a private crisis for Jackson which they planned to exploit to further their own party fortunes. Webster declaimed in the Senate that the military appropriations Jackson had requested would give him the power of a military dictator, and he would not vote them even if the enemy were battering down the gates of the capital. Adams was outraged. Fully convinced of the justice of Jackson's course, he considered this partisan trifling with the needs of the nation in a foreign crisis an abomination. Largely through his efforts, the House voted strong backing for Jackson's policy. Adams regarded this vote as his first parliamentary victory, and he wrote exultingly to his son Charles: "I breasted them all, and after thirteen hours of debate closed with a vote of two hundred and ten *ayes* for my Resolution and not one solitary *nay.* . . . I obtained in the House of Representatives a triumph unparalleled in the history of the country, while at the same time, it was the immediate cause of my exclusion from the Senate of the United States."

Charles did not share his father's enthusiasm over this victory, which he thought Adams had greatly exaggerated to conceal his disappointment at being denied the Senate seat. Adams's nonpartisan stand on the French claims was viewed by Whig leaders as another proof of his party unreliability, which dated back to the embargo crisis under Jefferson. It was now clear that in this latest instance of party irregularity, combined with his defeat for the governorship of Massachusetts a few years earlier, Adams's chances for a return to the Presidency had completely vanished.

Charles could see no reason for his father to remain in the House of Representatives. There had been neither dishonor nor discredit in his father's legislative activities, but there was also no striking justification for the former President and the nation's foremost statesman to occupy an inferior post in Congress. Adams was now seventy years old. For a moment, he almost yielded to his son's entreaties to return to Quincy and retirement. But only for a moment! For the old man knew that politics was as necessary for his bloodstream as his red corpuscles; without it he would soon wither and die. Charles might do or think as he pleased, but he would remain in Congress as long as the people wanted him there. John Quincy apparently had no premonition of the great role he was to play in the monumental struggle against slavery. But had he not followed his deepest instincts he would not have been present to answer that call.

13

The Righteous Man
Finds a Righteous Cause

IN THE EARLY YEARS of the American Revolution when John Quincy was barely seven years old, a conspiracy of Boston Negroes was uncovered by the patriots. The carefully guarded news, bearing an ominous portent for the revolutionary cause, reached Abigail Adams. A group of slaves, it appears, had prevailed upon an Irishman to draft a petition to Governor Thomas Gage, commander of British occupation forces, in which they offered to bear arms against the revolutionaries in return for his pledge to liberate them from bondage when the troubles had subsided. Abigail was troubled and indignant, not at the Negroes but at the morally indefensible position in which slavery placed the patriot cause. "I wish most sincerely," she wrote John Adams, "there was not a slave in the province. It always appeared a most iniquitous scheme to me—to fight ourselves for what we are daily robbing and plundering from those who have as good a right to freedom as we have. You know my mind upon this subject."

John Quincy must also have known his mother's mind, for she had considered awareness of the issues of the day an indispensable part of his education. In later life, there were to be many occasions when he was stung by the inconsistency of his country's claims with its practices. How could a nation which had fought a war for the rights of man justify the total denial of these rights to human beings it had condemned to the status of personal property? Again and again, in his various capacities as diplomat, Senator, Secretary of State and President, in dealing with foreign nations he was to find the just cause he defended tarnished by the stigma of slavery. But for Adams, as for many of his contemporaries, the problem remained one of private conscience rather than of public debate. In the early years of the republic the slave system, which had few defenders even among slaveholders, was considered a transient phenomenon that would gradually disappear. Even the more pessimistic preferred to wait, doubting that public sentiment could be rallied for abolition. As a senator, Adams himself had seen his Constitutional amendment for the rescinding of the three-fifths rule of representation die for lack of support. The issue seemed neither timely nor profitable for politicians.

As Adams began his Congressional career a great change was transforming the South. Cotton had replaced rice and tobacco as the money crop and was rapidly becoming the principal source of wealth and power below the Mason-Dixon line. Soon two-thirds of the world's supply of cotton was grown in the Southern states. The admission of five new states, Louisiana, Mississippi, Alabama, Missouri and Arkansas, extended the boundaries of the Cotton Kingdom as far south as the Gulf of Mexico and westward to the Mississippi.

This agricultural shift brought decline and decay to the rural aristocracy of the Virginia tidewater region, with its leisurely, unhurried and cultured way of life and its paternalistic and often humane treatment of the slaves. It also resulted in a startling revival of the slave system. From a domestic servant and a general farm laborer the slave was reshaped into a means of production in great factories in the field. Cotton, grown over large areas, could be efficiently produced by gang labor, which could be kept marching across the fields, plowing, hoeing, or picking according to the season. The slave population soared, increasing in the decade from 1830 to 1840 by 76 percent in Alabama and by 197 percent in Mississippi. One-crop agriculture was highly wasteful, quickly exhausting the soil and obliging the plantation owner to seek newer and richer lands in the Southwest, but it was also immensely lucrative. A Negro hand in Texas, for example, could produce ten bales of cotton, which would sell for $400 in New Orleans and realize for his owner a net profit of $300.

The economic growth of nations has rarely been achieved except at the cost of great human suffering. During the industrial revolution in England, for example, women and children labored from sunup to sundown in the mills and mines for a bare pittance and lived under conditions of unbelievable squalor and disease. The life of workers at the dawn of the factory system of New England and the Middle Atlantic states was only slightly better. But not since antiquity had there existed as hideous and vicious, as immoral and inhuman a labor system as that to which the Negro bondsmen of the South were subjected.

The white man had immigrated to the New World of his own free will to escape religious or political persecution. The black man, kidnapped and sold into bondage on the coasts of Africa, was torn from his home and transported to America like cattle in the infamous slavers which could be recognized miles away at sea by the stench of the unburied dead still chained to the living.

When the international slave trade was finally outlawed, Negroes were bred for sale on slave farms in Virginia and Kentucky, whose annual combined human production reached almost thirteen thousand "units." From the farms, the Negroes were shipped to slave auctions in the principal cities of the South. Purchases were made without regard for family ties, separating mothers from their children, husbands and wives, brothers and sisters. They were then either transported to the plantations by ship or marched overland in coffles, which were slave caravans. A slave gang being driven from the upper to the lower South was a familiar sight. The men were chained in pairs to prevent their escape while the women walked with their children, carrying their possessions in large bundles; slavedealers riding on horseback and armed with long whips herded them on their way.

On the plantations the slave received the minimum necessities to maintain life and the most rudimentary medical care; he was frequently flogged, for punishment was a calculated means to maintain discipline and especially output. The slave was the human machinery for the coining of profits, but he differed from other machinery in that he could stand greater abuse, required less attention, and harsh and brutal treatment did not necessarily lead to a breakdown. Plantation life was permeated with fear and terror, cruelty and hatred. The only hope for a change was death or flight. Runaway slaves were numerous. Those who were not driven back by hunger and privation from their hideouts in the swamps were tracked down by bloodhounds and professional posses of manhunters. From time to time a desperate slave insurrection would occur. The most famous of these revolts was led by Nat Turner in the summer of 1831 in Southampton, Virginia. It sent a chill of fear and panic throughout the white South. Although the uprising was quickly and savagely repressed, it marked a milestone in the history of slavery.

Throughout the Southern states repressive laws known as the Black Codes were enacted. It became unlawful to teach a slave to read or write. He was not permitted to stray from the plantation without a written pass, nor could Negroes congregate to hear a religious sermon or assemble for dancing or social purposes without the presence of a white person. He could not own firearms, horses, horns or drums, nor could he administer medicine to a white person or work in a pharmacy or a printing shop. Death was the penalty for plotting to revolt, suspected arson or rape and Negroes were prohibited from testifying in a court of law against a white person. Freemen were harassed and persecuted; Negro sailors were quarantined on their ships in Southern ports.

Lured by profits and frightened by visions of revolt, Southern thinking on slavery underwent a drastic change. The illustrious Virginians of the revolutionary generation—Washington, Jefferson, Madison, Patrick Henry and others, most of them slaveholders themselves—had all favored emancipation. In the succeeding years it was not uncommon for a slaveholder to consider the manumission of his slaves as the most important item of his will. Now the embarrassment and the defensive apology for the "temporary evil" were gone. Slavery was openly, aggressively upheld as good and just.

Meanwhile, Northern opinion was also changing—in the opposite direction. Opposition to slavery was stimulated by an awakening of the public conscience, spurred by a religious revival and a movement for social reforms that swept the North in the decade of the 1830's. The success of the abolitionists in the British Isles, whose efforts had been crowned in 1833 by the emancipation of the slaves in the West Indies, further encouraged the American antislavery movement. With a new sense of urgency, it now openly espoused the cause of abolition in place of its previous more moderate policy of attempting to enlist the support of the slaveholders in a scheme for the recolonization of the Negroes in Africa. The movement found its ethical purpose in the Holy Scriptures, its political ideals in the Declaration of Independence and its economic roots in the fears of Northern capitalists and farmers at the extension of slavery. The ranks of the abolitionists swelled with thousands of new adherents. In 1835, the Anti-Slavery Society counted some 27,000 members; three years later its membership soared to 250,000, with the number of its societies expanding from 235 to 1,350. Hardly a city, town or hamlet of the North was unrepresented.

Education and propaganda were the principal tools of the

abolitionists. They wanted to persuade public opinion, North and South, of the evils of slavery, to alert the people to the dangers of a divided nation in which the poisoned weeds of Southern tyranny would eventually choke the plant of Northern freedom. The pen, they never tired of repeating, was mightier than the sword. The slaveholders feared public controversy as a mortal peril to the "peculiar institution." Besides the effects of such a debate in the North, there were too many white men in the South who owned no slaves and who suffered from the arrogant rule of the plantation owners to risk a free discussion. Slavery had to be kept out of the marketplace of ideas even if it meant the suppression of free speech. The right to dissent from the prevailing opinion was soon throttled in the Southern states. In North Carolina, and later in Virginia, circulating publications which questioned the justice of slavery was punishable by imprisonment, a lockup in the public pillory, or whipping; death was the penalty for a second offense. In Louisiana any utterance "from bar, bench or stage" which might "produce discontent or insubordination among Negroes" was declared a crime. Northern liberals in Southern or border states found in possession of abolitionist literature were whipped and jailed. Mobs in the border states smashed the presses of antislavery publications.

When free speech was effectively stifled in the South, the slaveholders reached out to gag the North. The mayor of Savannah wrote the mayor of Boston urging the arrest and imprisonment of David Walker, a free Negro, who had written a pamphlet exhorting the slaves to fight for freedom. (With this exception, antislavery literature was directed exclusively to white men.) The governor of Virginia demanded that the governor of New York suppress the abolitionist publication *The Liberator*. An appointee of the Massachusetts legislature sent to Georgia to investigate the quarantining of Negro sailors was expelled from the state.

The most stringent curb on civil liberties was a bill presented to the Senate with the support of President Jackson and his Postmaster General to prohibit the circulation of "incendiary" publications through the mails. It was occasioned by the seizure in Charleston of a shipload of abolitionist literature addressed to the respectable citizens of Charleston, including ministers of all denominations. Strangely enough, the bill was defeated by the efforts of Calhoun, who believed it a violation of states' rights and suggested that the prerogative of censorship ·be left to the states. While the debate was proceeding a mob hauled the pamphlets into the street and burned them.

To counteract these restrictions the abolitionists began to focus attention on Congress as a forum for presenting their views. In those days the proceedings of the national legislature were the center of wide public interest. People were intensely, passionately concerned about politics, because it so closely affected their lives and future, but also because there were no mass diversions, no sports or entertainment to distract their attention. The speeches of a Webster, a Clay or a Calhoun were followed and talked about with the same intensity that is today reserved for a World Series match or a television program. To force a discussion of slavery in Congress was a means second to none for the abolitionists to mold public opinion.

The petition became the keystone of the abolitionist strategy. It constituted a kind of direct dialogue between the people and their representatives. The first scattered abolitionist petitions, signed by citizens of Northern communities, begged Congress to enact legislation to prohibit slavery and the slave trade in the District of Columbia. They considered the presence of 6,000 slaves in Washington disgraceful and the trade in human flesh in the shadow of the Capitol a national scandal. Adams's first act in Congress in December 1831 was the presentation of fifteen such petitions addressed to him by a group of Pennsylvania Quakers. He himself was not in accord with their plea. Despite his abhorrence of slavery and his conviction that there could be no permanence to a Union divided between free and slave communities, he believed the proposal would only create ill will and mutual hatred. The issue then was still not at the boiling point.

Three years later, as the pace of abolitionist activity quickened, the situation became greatly altered. Petitions were more numerous and more aggressive in tone, more outspoken in their condemnation of slavery. The proslavery men and their allies answered these demands with a concerted effort to suppress the right of petition. Representative Wise of Virginia laid down the precept that slavery was guaranteed by the Constitution, and that any attack upon it by Northerners was an attack upon "the institutions of our country, our safety and our welfare." Pinckney of South Carolina followed with a three-part resolution: 1. that Congress had no Constitutional power to interfere with slavery in the states; 2. that Congress should not interfere with slavery in the District of Columbia; 3. that all petitions concerning slavery or its abolition should be automatically tabled without being discussed, referred or printed. This was the first gag rule, a clear interdiction of the right of free speech in Congress.

The gag was imposed forthwith. Debate on the resolutions was shut off when their proponents had finished speaking. Twice Adams, defying the Speaker's arbitrary rulings, was shouted down and rapped out of order. But the ex-President was not so easily silenced. A master of parliamentary tactics, he contrived to voice his opposition to the first part of the resolution after it had already been adopted. Did anyone believe, he challenged, that Congress would stand by impotently while the expansionist drive of the slave states to conquer Texas, Mexico and Cuba involved the nation in war with foreign powers and resulted in a servile insurrection or civil war on its own territory? To save the Union under such circumstances, he declared prophetically, the war powers of Congress enabled it to interfere with the domestic affairs of the states and, if necessary, to fully emancipate the slaves. A quarter of a century later, Abraham Lincoln would find in Adams's speech a model for his immortal Emancipation Proclamation.

In the 1836 Congress, however, there were only eight men who dared to vote with Adams for this Constitutional principle. On the second resolution, urging Congress not to interfere with slavery in the District of Columbia, he asked to be excused from voting. The first name called in the roll call on the third section, the gag rule, was that of John Quincy Adams. The old man rose from his seat and shouted:

"I hold the resolution to be in direct violation of the Constitution of the United States, of the rules of this House, and of the rights of my constituents."

Speaker Polk furiously rapped his gavel, and the resolution passed by a vote of 117 to 68, but it was clear that no gag would seal the lips of the man who was to be slavery's most redoubtable adversary.

The South had won a Pyrrhic victory. In striking down the right of petition, it had linked the antislavery cause with the defense of civil liberties. This was the view Adams maintained in face of abolitionist disappointment with his stand on the prohibition of slavery in the District of Columbia. To fight on that ground, he contended, was to fight a losing battle, for votes could not be won for it in Congress, nor support mustered in the country at large. If the attitude of the North toward slavery was generally one of indifference, it was jealous of its rights, uneasy and suspicious at the tightening grip of the South on the federal government. In rallying the North to protect its liberties, the battle with the slaveholders would therefore be most effectively engaged. This flanking strategy urged by Adams was soon adopted, and with telling effect, by the abolitionist movement.

The dynamic, driving leadership of Theodore Weld, who later became a close associate of Adams, galvanized the antislavery forces into action. Seventy men (the number sent out in Biblical times to convert the world to Christianity), sifted from scores of candidates, trained and indoctrinated to meet all contingencies, were sent across the country to proselytize for abolitionism. They worked with unceasing perseverance, with the devotion of Christian martyrs. They were lynched and mobbed, branded on their foreheads and backs as "traitors, madmen, incendiaries, and fanatics." Undaunted, their indefatigable activity continued; existing organizations flourished, new societies sprang up. A network of a thousand branches stretching from New England to Ohio, with friends in Michigan, Indiana and Illinois, was directed toward a single objective: the petition.

The petitions were brief, usually one sentence, for under the gag rule they could not be read but only presented by subject: abolition in the District of Columbia; against the annexation of Texas; outlaw slavery in the territories; suppress the domestic slave trade; refuse statehood to Florida under slavery.

Everyone was solicited for a signature. "Follow the farmer to his field," the petitioner was exhorted, "the woodchopper to the forest. Hail the shopkeeper from behind his counter; call the clerk from his desk; stop the waggoner with his team; forget not the matron, ask her daughter. Let no frown deter, no repulse baffle. Explain, discuss, argue, persuade."

By the time Congress convened in 1837, petitions were pouring into Washington like an avalanche. They occupied the entire time of several clerks; they were stowed by "waggonloads" in the antechambers.

Although there were no direct ties between Adams and the Anti-Slavery Society, he rapidly became the pivotal figure in the siege against the gag rule. A growing volume of petitions were addressed to him or were redirected to his attention to keep them from falling into the hands, and wastebaskets, of Northern Congressmen who were described as "trucklers to Southern power." Other Congressmen might present petitions as a token gesture to their constituents, but for Adams it was the battle of a lifetime. He attacked the problem with all his intellectual resources, his unswerving moral convictions, and amazing residues of physical strength for a body that had weathered threescore and ten years. With infinite ingenuity and bulldog tenacity he tore at the Southern defenses. His purpose was to batter down the gag rule, to force a discussion of slavery by linking it with the fight for the right of petition, to provoke, harass, irritate and challenge the Southerners to debate publicly the merits of slavery versus freedom. It was a dangerous game, and Adams compared it with "a walk on the edge of a precipice."

Adams was not an orator in the grand style of a Clay or a Webster. Although he had been a professor of rhetoric at Harvard, he entered Congress with little experience in extemporaneous speaking. Nervous, uncertain of his next sentence, forgetting half his points, his first speeches were an ordeal. It was in the thick of battle that he found his voice and won the nickname "Old Man Eloquent." His spare oratory, in sharp contrast to the elaborate rhetoric of many politicians at the time, became a formidable weapon. The righteous man had found a righteous cause. Restraints and compromises imposed by political considerations, concern for career and reasons of state had fallen away like so many chains; he had first to be free himself, it seemed, before he could wage war for the freedom of his fellow man. He had reversed the familiar cycle of the politician's life, which begins with the youthful agitator ready to battle the world for noble and radical ideals and ends with the cautious elder statesman, clinging to stability, order and the *status quo*. Adams, the staid diplomat, the careful politician, the conservative President—such was his youth and middle age—was concluding his political life as a tribune of the people, a foe of slavery in the South and an enemy of complacency in the North, a proponent of radical change who asked and gave no quarter.

14

Old Man Eloquent
and The Right to Petition

MONDAY WAS the day reserved by the House for receiving petitions. As the roll was called in geographical order beginning with the Northeast, Adams of Massachusetts was usually the first to be recognized, for in addition to petitions from his own state, most of those from Maine, New Hampshire and Vermont were directed to him. Looking for all the world like a retired banker, the bald, potbellied old man was on his feet when the Twentieth Congress assembled on January 9, 1837. He was anxious to take advantage of a brief interim before the reimposition of the gag rule shut off all debate. In his hand were three petitions bearing some 375 signatures from the women of his own Plymouth district and from neighboring Dorchester pleading for the abolition of slavery in the District of Columbia. Adams begged the House to listen to their request.

In defiant response, Southern representatives and their Northern allies immediately voted to lay the petition on the table without reading it. Adams then produced the second petition and began to read:

"Impressed with the sinfulness of slavery, and keenly aggrieved by its existence in a part of our Country over which—"

"Mr. Speaker!" shouted Pinckney of South Carolina. He demanded that Adams be called to order under the provisions of the gag rule. The Speaker, James Polk, had to acknowledge that the rule was not yet in force, but he testily instructed Adams:

"You have a right to make a brief statement of the contents of the petition."

"I am doing so, Sir," Adams countered.

"Not in the opinion of the Chair," Polk insisted.

"I was at the point of the petition," Adams reminded him and resumed his reading:

"—keenly aggrieved by its existence in a part of our Country over which Congress possesses exclusive jurisdiction in all cases whatever—"

"Order! Order!" rang out from all parts of the hall, but Adams read on:

"—immediately to abolish slavery in the District of Columbia—"

"A point of order!" demanded Chambers of Kentucky, and as the clamor rose throughout the chamber, Polk yielded to his Southern confederates and ordered the member from Plymouth to be seated. Lowering himself slowly into his chair as if to comply with the Speaker's instructions, the old man went on reading with greater force and emphasis on each syllable:

"—and to declare every human being free who sets foot on its soil—"

"Take your seat, Mr. Adams!" Polk shouted, bringing down his gavel heavily on the rostrum.

Immediately Chambers was on his feet insisting that the Speaker rule that a statement of the contents of a petition did not include a reading of the text. Polk agreed, but Adams challenged his ruling, and this precipitated a disorderly procedural debate. This was more than Adams could have hoped for. He had already read the bulk of his petition; now the parliamentary tangle would permit him to complete it. He magnanimously offered to withdraw his appeal if the gentle-man from Kentucky would consent to his reading the few remaining words of the petition; it would be briefer that way than if he made his own summary. Chambers had to assent, and Adams concluded:

"—the petitioners respectfully announce their intention *to present the same petition yearly* before this honorable body that it might at least be a memorial to the holy cause of freedom."

The same petition every year! That was the crowning stroke.

Tumultuous cries for order rang out as Adams sat down, this time of his own accord. It was a good day's work. But no sooner had the House voted on the disposition of the peti-tion, than Adams was on his feet again to present another petition. It was quickly tabled, and a few days later the gag rule was reenacted.

Adams's single-handed duel against a majority of Congress was now in full tilt. While he prodded and pried, seeking out the weak points in the proslavery defenses, his enemies schemed to catch him off guard and then to drive him into a corner where there would be no escape from their vindictive wrath. On petition day, two weeks later, Adams presented twenty-three petitions. All of them were tabled without being read. Twenty-three times he moved that they first be read, and each time the speaker ruled his motion out of order; twenty-three times Adams appealed the Speaker's decision to the House, and each time the body upheld the Speaker. A conservative Northern newspaper deplored that the "Massa-chusetts Madman" should be permitted to persist in present-ing abolition petitions. But Adams persisted—because there was method in his "madness."

While pondering some new stratagem to pierce the gag rule, he found in his mail an unusual petition. It appeared to be a message from slaves who had scrawled their "X" marks beneath a text penned by a literate person. Recognizing the telltale signs of a malicious contrivance intended to explode in his hands, Adams decided to gamble dangerously and beat the devil at his own game. On February 9, he juggled the bomb before the full view of the House. Would the Speaker make a ruling, Adams queried, on the disposition of this paper purporting to come from slaves and which he had been requested to present? Did it come within the scope of the prohibition against the reading of petitions dealing with slavery? He would relinquish the paper when the decision was rendered.

Confronted with the first slave petition ever to come before Congress, Polk turned in bewilderment to the House for advice and direction.

"Expel him! Expel him!" Southern hotspurs shouted from their seats.

Waddy Thompson of South Carolina launched into a frenzied tirade. "The sanctuary of age," he roared, "is not to be violated lightly, but when that sanctuary is used to throw poisoned arrows, it ceases to be sacred." Adams was inciting the slaves to insurrection; this was a crime, he warned, for which the gentleman from Massachusetts could be indicted before the grand jury of the District of Columbia.

Thompson's threat was followed by a flood of angry accusations. The ex-President, said one Southerner, was an unconscionable tool of "incendiary fanatics." He was insulting the South, and should be brought to book, demanded another. Threatening the Union! echoed a third. Resolutions of censure came pouring down. One was introduced by Thompson; it was amended by Dixon Lewis of Alabama, amended again by Haynes of Georgia. Suitable punishment had to be inflicted on the representative from Plymouth, the mouthpiece of the "barbarian abolitionists," for presenting a petition from slaves demanding their freedom, for trampling on the decorum of the House, for trifling with the dignity of its members, for violating its sacred rules.

Calmly, patiently, without betraying the slightest emotion, Adams waited for a lull in the storm. Then with great deliberation he proceeded to dissect the motions of censure. He had been accused of presenting a petition on behalf of slaves, although in fact he had presented no such petition but had merely inquired of the Speaker regarding its disposition. "If such a question . . . asked of the Speaker . . . subjects me to an indictment by a grand jury, to conviction by a petit jury, and to an infamous penitentiary cell—I ask you not what freedom is left to your representatives in Congress, but what freedom of speech, of the press, and of thought is left TO YOU?" He had been accused of presenting a petition of slaves for the abolition of slavery. That part of the censure resolution would have to be altered, he informed his would-be prosecutors, because the paper was a plea for the *retention* of slavery and an argument against abolition!

There was consternation in the Dixie camp. They had lit a fuse to blow up John Quincy Adams, but the bomb had exploded in their own backyard. For a moment their rage was uncontained. New motions were drafted to censure and expel their exasperating foe for contempt of Congress, for disrespect to its members.

Wiser heads soon prevailed. A new set of resolutions was introduced; added to the dozen which had been buried, the total now came to fifteen. The new motions resolved: 1. that any member who introduces a slave petition "regardless of the feelings of the House" and the "rights of the southern states" would be considered "unfriendly to the Union"; 2. "that slaves do not possess the right of petition secured to the people of the United States by the Constitution"; 3. that all further proceedings against Adams be dropped as he had "solemnly disclaimed all design of doing anything disrespectful to this House. . . ." The last was a face-saving device implying, contrary to the facts, that Adams regretted his action.

At this point, an Ohio Congressman, suddenly concerned over the possible reactions of his constituents, moved to table the whole matter. Adams, demanding the right to be heard in his own defense, vigorously opposed the motion. This time he was sustained by an overwhelming majority of the House.

The tables had been turned in an unforgettable and dramatic scene. The accused became the accuser, the defendant became the prosecutor. In the name of the slaves, Adams cracked his most merciless rhetorical whip over the slave-drivers.

"There is not a word in the Constitution of the United States," Adams declared, "excluding petitions from slaves. . . . Shall the slave not be permitted to cry for mercy? to plead for pardon? to utter the shriek of perishing nature for relief? . . . Sir, the framers of the Constitution would have repudiated the idea that they were giving to the people the right of petition." His voice rose in indignation. "No, Sir. That right God gave to the whole human race when he made them *men*—the right of prayer, by asking a favor of another. The doctrine is that this right belongs to humanity—that the right of petition is the right of prayer not depending on the condition of the petitioner. No despot of any age or clime has ever denied this humble privilege to the poorest or the meanest of human creatures. The Sultan of Turkey cannot walk the streets of Constantinople and refuse to receive a petition from the vilest slave, who stands to meet him as he passes by." The House was extraordinarily quiet when Adams cried out: "It will be a sad day when it is entered upon the journals of this House that we will under no circumstances receive the petition of slaves. When you begin to limit the right, where shall it stop?"

Adams had been attacked for merely inquiring whether Congress would hear a slave petition. Now he was standing before that same Congress, ungagged and unrepentant, openly championing the rights of slaves, defiantly linking the unrecognized prerogatives of Negroes with the hard-pressed rights of the white man. Not a voice was raised to shout him down, not a solitary interjection, not the slightest query. Well, he would make them talk. He would instruct the Southern paragons of courtesy in some of the rudiments of human decency.

There was not a word of truth in the censure resolutions proposed by the gentlemen from South Carolina and Alabama, Adams charged. The next time, he cautioned them, they try to censure a man "who never gave them the slightest cause for offense . . . they should first be careful to pay attention to the facts."

The stinging rebuke brought the two men to their feet. Lewis of Alabama explained that he had entered the House in the midst of the excitement, and had taken it for granted that the slaves were petitioning through Adams for abolition. Naturally, he would never have offered his resolution had he known the object of the petition. Adams acknowledged the explanation with a slight note of sarcasm. "He took for granted what happened not to be true." So much for Lewis.

Now it was Thompson's turn. Let him explain his threat to bind Adams over to the grand jury for allegedly inciting slaves to insurrection. Thompson cringed: "Had I known the character of the petition, I certainly would not have made those remarks. They would have applied to an abolition petition; they do not apply to the gentleman from Massachusetts."

Adams was not appeased. The explanation was unacceptable. Had he actually presented the imagined petition, Adams pursued, for no other cause than "for words spoken in this House" Thompson would have expelled him and "invoked on my head the vengeance of the grand jury of this district." Thompson, he said, was a representative of the slaveholders, "and I should like to be informed how many other there are of such representatives on this floor who endorse that sentiment."

"I do not," was heard from several voices in the hall.

The old man was unrelenting. "Is it to be tolerated, that, for anything a member says on this floor, though it were blasphemy or treason, he is to be held accountable and punished by the grand and petit juries of this District and not by this House? If that is the doctrine of the slaveholding representatives of this floor, let it, in God's name, go forth, and let us see what the people of this nation think of such a sentiment and of those who make such an avowal."

"I will *not* endorse it," Henry Wise, leader of the Southern bloc, interjected. "If I believed the members of this House were amenable in any way to the juries of this district I would not hold a seat here for one moment. . . ."

Lacking the Virginian's shrewdness, Thompson blurted out in all candor: "In South Carolina any member of the legislature who presented a petition from slaves would be liable to indictment by a grand jury."

"That may do for Southern legislatures," Adams thundered, ". . . and if it is the law of South Carolina . . . God Almighty receive my thanks that I am not a citizen of South Carolina. [Great agitation in the House]. . . . Let that gentleman, let every member ask his heart, with what confidence, with what boldness, with what firmness he would give utterance to his opinions on this floor, if for every word, for a mere question asked of the Speaker involving human freedom and the rights of man, he was liable to be tried as a felon or an incendiary, and sent to the penitentiary! . . . Such is the avowed doctrine of the gentleman from South Carolina; such are his notions of freedom of speech and civil liberty.

"Did the gentleman think he could frighten me from my purpose by his threat of a grand jury? If that was his object, let me tell him *he mistook his man*. I am not to be frightened from the discharge of a duty by the indignation of the gentleman from South Carolina, nor by all the grand juries of this universe!"

Old Man Eloquent's victory was almost complete. His enemies were in full rout. They tried to table the motions and

adjourn, but failed. They carried the second resolution de-
priving the slave of the right to petition, but they failed to
carry the first resolution, and the oblique attack on Adams
in the third resolution went down to a resounding defeat;
only 21 of 126 votes were cast in its favor.

The slaveholders had suffered a stinging defeat. It was the
first time that the Northern alliance with the slave South
had been severed; only three Northern Congressmen had
voted for the indirect censure of Adams. At the very moment
the Senate had branded any interference with slavery where
it existed as an attempt to destroy the Union, the House,
goaded by Adams, had refused to stigmatize the presentation
of a petition from slaves as "unfriendly to the Union."

When Adams refused to be intimidated by threats of political disgrace and even imprisonment, his enemies resorted to
threats of bodily injury. The first of a long series of such
threats was contained in a letter addressed to Adams at the
conclusion of the debate in Congress. At the top of the page
next to a drawing in red of a raised arm holding a bowie
knife were the words: "Vengeance is mine, say the South!"
Directly below were a whip and lash with the caption: "Flog
and spare not!" Then followed the savage text:

". . . Your endeavors to agitate the question of abolition
upon each succeeding week shows the blackness of your
heart. . . . *The rod is cut and seasoned that will make your
old hide smart* for your insidious attempt on Southern rights.
I [it was signed by "Dirk Hatteraik"] send you this as a caution, as your course will be watched, and if ever you dare attempt vindicate abolition again you will be *lynched,* if it has
to be done by *drawing* you from your *seat* in the *House by
force.* So be on your guard. The author of this is now on his
way to Washington with *others* able and *determined to fulfill their threats.*"

In the midst of these vicious attacks Adams was heartened
by messages of support and encouragement. "Go on then
Sage of Quincy!" exhorted an admirer from Boston. "Fear

not Southern insolence. Defend our petitions and we in turn will defend and sustain you. You have never been welcomed home with more heartfelt gratitude, and you will always be so long as you possess the courage and patriotism you have lately manifested. Our legislature has sustained you. Yes, and the people will not only sustain you, but love you."

Such letters and the supporting resolution of the Massachusetts legislature were symptoms of a political reawakening of New England. The heroic battle of a native son against the new tyranny was stirring the conscience of the people whose forebears had participated in the Boston Tea Party and fought at Lexington and Concord. Old Man Eloquent had leaped into national prominence. Although his close friends and immediate family continued to object to his involvement in politics, his constituents encouraged his course of action. He had become the nation's great champion of civil liberties. It was a new role for the son of the man who had signed the Alien and Sedition Acts. It was a role the abolitionists heartily approved, but they could not understand why he would not take a forthright position for the abolition of slavery.

Adams's heart was with the abolitionists, but his ear was closer to the ground. If a frontal attack on slavery would find little response, the people were nevertheless prepared to defend their rights. He prevailed upon the abolitionists to shift their sights farther South, from the futile effort to abolish slavery in the District of Columbia to the line of the Rio Grande. Almost everyone in the north had signed a petition against the annexation of Texas, and these were petitions outside the scope of the gag rule. Texas was chosen as the next front of the antislavery struggle.

15

Texas and the
Slaveholders' Conspiracy

THE VAST PROVINCE of Texas had virtually no European settlements when Mexico won its independence from Spain in 1821. Besides the Indians roaming the plains, some 3,000 persons of Spanish origin, who clustered around the ports and the mission towns, were its only inhabitants. The rich alluvial soil and the far-flung prairies, ideally suited to farming and cattle raising, were tempting to hardy, enterprising pioneers. When its plans for development of the area had failed for lack of resources and emigrants, the Mexican government opened the land to foreign settlement. Offering liberal terms of immigration and land disposal, it invited Anglo-American immigrants to populate the empty prairies. A land rush, of considerable proportions for the time, began. By 1830 there were some 15,000 immigrants in Texas; five years later there were twice that many.

The new inhabitants were a heterogeneous group. In addition to industrious farmers seeking a better life on a new frontier, there were slaveowners, speculators, fortune hunters, scheming politicians and adventurers—the usual motley collection of men who chase the pot of gold at the end of the rainbow. They had come not to colonize but to take possession. They chafed under the absentee rule of a government which was represented on the territory by a few appointed officials and scattered garrisons of soldiers. They were impatient with laws and restrictions, which bridled their restless, competitive spirit. They were Protestants in a Catholic country; Anglo-Saxons who regarded the Latins as an inferior people.

This unsettled and worsening state of affairs alarmed the Mexican government. The people they had welcomed, disregarding laws, titles and deeds, seemed bent on ousting them as proprietors. The crisis came to a head in an unsuccessful attempt in 1825 to establish Texas as an independent republic. Fearing to lose control of their province, the Mexican congress passed a body of restrictive laws, chief among which were a ban on the importation of slaves, the expulsion of squatters who could not show title to their lands and the cancellation of land contracts which had not been fulfilled by promoters. These measures were of little or no use, for the government was in no position to enforce the laws. Mexico in the years after independence was a troubled and chaotic country. The government's efforts to cope with the problems left by Spanish rule gave rise to a continuing revolutionary ferment, with peons fighting for liberation from landowners and republicans seeking secular rule against the opposition of the clergy. Weak and corrupt governments, often dominated by military adventurers, rose and fell in rapid succession.

In 1834, at the culmination of a long struggle for power, General Santa Anna seized the reins of government. He moved at once to establish centralized control over the northern province and to compel respect for the long-dormant laws. These included a law abolishing slavery, passed in 1829, which planters had evaded for years under the guise of importing their slaves as "indentured servants." The storm signals went up in Texas. When Santa Anna denied a petition for local autonomy in November 1835, armed detachments of Texans launched an attack upon Mexican outposts and garrisons. By the end of the year, the last Mexican soldier was driven across the border, and the following March, Texas was proclaimed an independent republic. Now Santa Anna, at the head of a large army, swept northward to put down the rebellion. For a time he carried everything before him, inflicting a terrible defeat on the Texans in the bloody siege of the Alamo in San Antonio. The next month the tide of battle turned. An army of Texans, under General Sam Houston, shouting "Remember the Alamo," descended upon their foes on the banks of the San Jacinto River, massacring nearly half the Mexican army and capturing most of the survivors, including their general. To save himself from a firing squad, Santa Anna agreed to evacuate Texas and to prevail upon the Mexican government to recognize its independence.

Immediately upon its victory, the newly constituted Lone Star Republic applied for admission to the United States. On the face of it, nothing seemed more normal, more acceptable. Americans had settled a new country, they had wrested it in battle from a foreign power, and now they were generously offering to turn it over to their native land. In fact, the proposal was charged with dynamite. It would precipitate bitter political discord, lead to a war of conquest against Mexico, and finally plunge the United States into civil war.

The acquisition of Texas had been an objective of United States foreign policy since the days of the Florida purchase. John Quincy Adams, during his term in the White House, and later Andrew Jackson had attempted to prevail upon Mexico to sell Texas to the United States. In both instances the offer had been rejected as an offense to the national honor, and the American ambassadors, accused of meddling in internal Mexican politics, had been sent home. Andrew Jackson was far from neutral during the Texas rebellion. Its leader, Sam Houston, was a Tennessean and an old friend of the President's. Houston knew that if he could not expect open support, Jackson would do nothing to impede his plans. Jackson went so far as to order General Gaines and a regiment of United States troops to occupy Nacogdoches in Mexican territory during the hostilities in Texas. This was an open breach of the boundary treaty between the two countries.

There was little opposition to these expansionist designs until they became associated in the minds of Northerners with a further aggrandizement of the slave power. The reasons for Southern eagerness for the annexation of Texas were all too evident. The Cotton Kingdom coveted the rich lands to enhance its economic strength, to replace the exhausted soil in the east. At least four or five new states would be carved out of the former Mexican province, resulting in a massive increase of Southern representation in both houses of Congress. Annexation was also an insurance against the establishment of a free-state republic which could become a haven for runaway slaves from Southern plantations.

There was a growing conviction among Northerners that the Texas issue masked an ominous slaveholders' conspiracy. They believed that the annexation of Texas would disrupt the balance of power in the Union, giving the South a commanding position in the federal government and the power to involve the United States in wars of conquest with Latin American countries. Two circumstances seemed to confirm these suspicions. One was a clause in the constitution of Texas nullifying the Mexican law abolishing slavery and enjoining the legislature from ever proclaiming the liberation of the slaves. The other was the fact that the initial sponsors of the Texas application for admission to the Union were slaveholding states: Mississippi, Alabama and Tennessee. The antislavery forces and a segment of Northern Whigs quickly united to forestall Southern plans and block the annexation. John Quincy Adams became the chief spokesman for this group.

The ex-President had always been an expansionist. He had supported the Louisiana Purchase at the cost of his Senator-

"Remember the Alamo" became the battle cry of Texans in their struggle against Mexico.

ial career. He had negotiated the Transcontinental Treaty with Spain, which extended the nation's boundaries to the Sabine River in eastern Texas and the Pacific Ocean in the Northwest. Later he took an uncompromising stand against England in the Oregon dispute. Adams had justified this empire building as the extension of a higher civilization and its republican institutions into new territory. If he drew the line at Texas it was because the annexation of a land which had reinstituted slavery where it had already been abolished did not meet these moral standards. Expansion in this case, he held, was little better than naked conquest, an ignominious role for a nation whose constitution proclaimed the rights of man. The end result would be the dissolution of the Union.

These thoughts were the theme of a masterful speech Adams delivered in Congress. It was made in opposition to a recommendation of the Committee on Foreign Affairs to extend recognition to Texas after the establishment of a workable civil government. The proposal had already passed the Senate, but Adams's philippic, a series of challenging interrogations hurled at the slaveholders, marshaled forty votes against the recommendation in the House.

Why do you covet Texas? he demanded. "Are you not large and unwieldy enough already? Do not two million square miles cover surface enough for the insatiable rapacity of your land jobbers? Have you not Indians enough to expel from the land of their fathers' sepulcher, and to exterminate? . . .

"Sir, is there not hatred enough between the races which compose your Southern population and the population of Mexico?" Hatred against the Indian whom "you are scourging from his land to the foot of the Rocky Mountains?" Hatred against the "American Negro of African origin, whom you are holding in cruel bondage? . . . Do you not as an Anglo-Saxon, slaveholding exterminator of Indians, from the bottom of your soul, hate the Mexican-Spaniard-Indian emancipator of slaves and abolisher of slavery? And do you

not think your hatred is not with equal cordiality returned? . . ."

War is bound to be the consequence: "A war of the races
—the Anglo-Saxon American pitted against the Moorish-
Spanish-Mexican American, a war between the Northern and
Southern halves of North America. . . ."

"And again I ask, what will be your *cause* in such a war?
Aggression, conquest and the re-establishment of slavery
where it had been abolished. In that war, sir, the banners of
freedom will be the banners of Mexico; and your banners, I
blush to speak the word, will be the banners of slavery."

Adams's blistering words stirred Northern opinion but
could not prevent recognition, which was extended a year
later, just before Jackson's term of office expired. Jackson
had hoped to use the captured Santa Anna as a tool to impose a treaty of recognition on Mexico. Santa Anna was willing enough, but the plan fell through when the Mexican
congress completely repudiated its erstwhile leader. Having
exchanged envoys with Texas, Jackson in his last request to
Congress belligerently demanded the powers of naval reprisal
to collect American claims against Mexico, which consisted
mostly of debts for supplies contracted by Mexico during its
revolution against Spain.

When the new Congress convened in December 1837,
Adams believed that the scheme for annexation was well advanced. Texas had voted for entry into the Union and had
sent a minister to Washington, who was negotiating with
President Van Buren, Jackson's successor. The Congressman
from Massachusetts, delegated by the fellow members from
his state, presented 190 petitions signed by some 20,000 persons, and a still larger number on behalf of his colleagues,
all of which protested any moves for annexation. The House
would have buried these petitions without discussion, as it
had so many others, were it not for a debate Adams provoked
over the committee to which the petitions were to be referred.

"Six out of the nine members of the Committee on For-

eign Affairs are slaveholders," Adams charged. That committee, he continued, could not give the petitions a proper
hearing. "The question is," declared Adams, launching directly into the issue itself, "whether a foreign nation (acknowledged as such in the most unprecedented and
extraordinary manner by this government), a nation 'damned
to everlasting fame' by the reinstitution of that detested system of slavery, after it had once been abolished within its
borders, should be admitted into union with a nation of
freemen. For, sir, that name, thank God, is still ours!"

There were interruptions from all parts of the hall. The
Speaker warned Adams to stay within the subject. A member
from South Carolina interjected that the time for this discussion had not yet come.

"Whether the question arise now or hereafter," Adams retorted, "is as immaterial to me as it can be to them; it must
come! . . . I do not think it will be forever smothered by the
previous question to lay it on the table . . . the same means
and argument, in spirit, which in other places have produced murder and arson. Yes, Sir, this same spirit which led
to the inhuman murder of Lovejoy in Alton—"

This reference to the lynching of the antislavery editor by
an Illinois mob brought shouts of "Order!" from the hall,
and Speaker Polk ordered Adams to take his seat. Adams appealed the ruling, promising not to mention Lovejoy's name.
The request was granted and the old warrior drove home his
final blow: "The annexation of Texas and the proposed war
with Mexico are one and the same thing."

The petitions were then tabled, without reference to a
committee, on the grounds that the government had already
declined the Texas request for admission to the Union because of its relations with Mexico. Sixty-eight votes were
counted against this Southern motion.

Several weeks later Adams found a new device to force a
renewal of the debate. It came in the form of a petition of
the New York Peace Society, signed mostly by women, to
halt the drift to war between the United States and Mexico

by submitting differences between the two nations to the arbitration of a third power or a world court. For the veteran diplomat who had always defended his country's cause against foreign powers, there was something momentous in this occasion:

"In all controversies in which this nation has been involved with foreign powers," he reminded his listeners, "I have invariably felt it my duty most scrupulously to ascertain the . . . right and wrong at issue . . . and it has always been, till now, my good fortune to be able to side with my own country; but now we are called upon to take a position which the sense of justice at the bottom of my soul will not permit me to approve. The wrong is upon our side and we are being drawn into war upon false and frivolous pretenses. . . .

"When there is an obvious intention to drive us into an iniquitous war, I will expose everything above ground and everything under ground. . . . No menace shall turn me from my course, be it of personal responsibility or be it of assassination, with both of which I have been threatened before now."

A three-hour debate followed between Adams and Benjamin Howard of Maryland, chairman of the Foreign Affairs Committee. The nub of their discussion was whether the Mexican government had indicated its willingness to arbitrate. No such proposition has reached our government, Howard affirmed. That does not mean that such a proposition does not exist, Adams persisted. Old Man Eloquent was too skillful for his interlocutor, and Howard finally conceded that there was, in fact, as Adams had alleged, a Mexican offer to compromise.

Congress may have been unmoved, but the general public, persuaded by Adams's brilliant dialectic of a hatching plot for war, demanded that the much inflated United States claims be arbitrated. As a Northern politician, Van Buren could ill afford to alienate so large a segment of Northern votes, and eventually he accepted the Mexican offer. On April 11, 1839, all United States claims, with the exception

of Texas, were turned over to a mixed commission whose
findings could be reviewed by an arbiter appointed by the
king of Prussia.

Adams had successfully avoided any immediate danger of
war with Mexico. He believed, however, that the administration was secretly intriguing behind the backs of Congress
with the Texas emissaries in Washington. The occasion to
"expose everything above ground and everything under
ground" soon arose. In addition to petitions protesting annexation signed by 100,000 persons, Congress had received
resolutions on the subject from various state legislatures—
from Rhode Island, Vermont, Massachusetts, Ohio and
Michigan deploring any extension of the slaveholders'
domain; from Tennessee and Alabama approving admission
of Texas as a reward for courage and as a measure which
would counterbalance Northern strength in Congress and
put an end to abolitionist agitation. Public concern was now
too intense to smother the issue by the gag rule system; the
various resolutions and remonstrances were referred, on
Adams's motion, to the Committee on Foreign Affairs with
instructions to report back to Congress. Whatever the report
of the stacked committee, Adams calculated, the issue would
be on the floor, where it could be grappled with.

In June 1838, less than a month before adjournment, the
committee submitted its recommendation. It had not considered or even read the petitions. It refused, however, to
advise any course of action because there was no Presidential proposition pending for the annexation of Texas or
its admission to the Union as a state. The committee members recommended, therefore, to table the petitions and to
terminate the work of the committee on the subject. If they
had hoped to thwart discussion by this device, they under-
estimated the determination and tactical brilliance of John
Quincy Adams. Through a series of maneuvers, Adams got
the floor and held it every morning until adjournment three
weeks later.

His filibuster was a merciless attack on the administration and a ringing indictment of slavery. Van Buren's policy, and Jackson's as well, he charged, was one of duplicity toward Mexico calculated to incite war and under cover of that war to annex Texas. The proofs of that intention were contained in documents which the President refused to make available to Congress; Jackson's instructions to his ministers in Mexico had been concealed from the House. If Texas remained an independent republic, Adams maintained, surrounded by two free nations like the United States and Mexico, slavery could not long exist within her borders. But if Texas were admitted to the Union as a slave state, "we shall have schools where our youth and children shall be taught that slaves are chattels, and slavery is a benevolent institution of God." In a tone of scathing contempt he said of the South, "I know well that the doctrine of the Declaration of Independence that 'all men are created equal' is there held as an incendiary doctrine, and deserves lynching. . . ."

The opposition tried repeatedly to silence Adams but failed each time to muster a majority. When Congress adjourned on July 9, 1838, Adams still held the floor, which entitled him to resume his speech when the body reconvened in December. But there was no need for a renewal of the oratorical marathon, for Adams had so thoroughly embarrassed the administration that it shelved its carefully contrived schemes. Advised of the impasse, the government of Texas instructed its envoys to withdraw the request for admission to the Union. Once again the slaveholders' designs had been checked, frustrated by the "Madman from Massachusetts" and buried under the pyramid of petitions from which they were exhumed only three years later.

Once again the measure of the ex-President's success was the fury it stirred in the South against him. When Congress reconvened that December, his mail bulged with threatening letters:

From Virginia: "Congress cannot get on with its busi-

ness . . . owing to your . . . abolition petitions. Some Gentlemen from this section are ready and anxious to pay a large
premium for the head of J. Q. Adams. . . ."

From Montgomery, Alabama: "Beware how you proceed,
Sir, or something will come over you as a thief in the night,
which may not be so agreeable."

From Augusta, Georgia: "For wishing a . . . Negro, alias
Whig to be seated in Congress hall, and to be considered an
equal to a white man in law and in justice . . . you will when
least expected, be shot down in the street, or your damned
guts will be cut out in the dark."

A fanatic from Kentucky warned Adams that the date for
his execution had been set for February 10, 1839. Another
threatened to shoot him in March, and a thug from "way
down in Alabama" promised to "cut your throat from Ear
to Ear" on the first of May.

Adams calmly entered these "bullying letters" in the
Congressional Record, and continued to present the petitions
directed to him, by the dozens and the hundreds, petitions
against annexation, against the internal slave trade, against
the admission of Florida as a slave state, for the recognition
of Haiti, for the rescinding of the gag rule.

There was no way Adams could silence his would-be as-
sassins, but he found the means to discipline the practice of
dueling frequently resorted to by members of Congress.
Congressman Graves of Kentucky took offense at what he
considered a slighting remark made by Congressman Jonathan Cilley of Maine in the course of a speech from the floor,
and demanded satisfaction on the field of honor. The duel-
ists, who harbored no ill will to one another, exchanged two
rounds of rifle fire without inflicting any injury. At this
point the seconds, and principally Representative Wise of
Virginia, insisted that the shooting continue for a third
round. Cilley, a young man and the father of three children,
was shot dead.

A wave of public indignation spread into the House itself;

indignant voices demanded that Graves and Wise be brought to justice. Adams held that such an action was in the province of the courts and not of Congress, but he joined with Senator Samuel Prentiss of Vermont in sponsoring an antidueling bill which provided heavy prison sentences for anyone delivering or accepting a challenge to a duel within the District of Columbia. The Prentiss-Adams bill was adopted into law on February 29, 1839. Wise had neither spoken nor voted on it.

But two years later, the Virginian complained bitterly to the House at the passing of this custom of Southern "chivalry." One member, he said, "is branded as a coward on the floor. The other says back that 'he is a liar.' And, Sir, there the matter will drop. *There will be no fight.*"

Adams was on his feet. "I maintain the contrary. I maintain it for the independence of this House, for my own independence . . . for the independence of the members of the Northern section of this country, who not only abhor dueling in theory, but in practice; in consequence of which members from other sections are perpetually insulting them on this floor under the impression that the insult will not be resented . . . and that 'there will be no fight'. . . . I am not willing to sit here any longer and see other members from my own section of the country, or those who may be my successors here, made subject to any such law as the law of the duelist. . . ."

Wise was silent as Adams concluded his denunciation of the barbaric custom, an "appendage to slavery." But the verbal duel between the two men would later resume under more dramatic circumstances.

16

The Amistad Case

THROUGHOUT HISTORY the pioneers in great struggles for human freedom have always had to battle apathy as well as opposition. When tyranny or oppression has existed for centuries, as was the case with slavery, the evil tends to be accepted as a normal part of life. Oppression that involves millions can be too big for the human mind to encompass. But a flagrant injustice perpetrated on a single individual, by narrowing the focus, often brings the suffering of masses into the popular vision. When the drama of a lonely, friendless, helpless human being, deprived of his rights and hunted down by a seemingly omnipotent state, is played out before the eyes of an entire nation, it enters history as a *cause célèbre*. The *Amistad* Case was such an instance in the struggle against slavery. The fact that it involved a group of persons rather than a solitary individual did not diminish its dramatic impact.

In April 1839, the Portuguese slaver *Tecora* transported a human cargo of Africans kidnapped on the Guinea coast to Cuba. Fifty-two Negroes survived the terrible Middle Passage and were then sold on the slave market in Havana. From beginning to end the operation was illegal. Slave trade was not only prohibited under Spanish law, but it was specifically stipulated that slaves imported into a Spanish colony were to be declared free in the first port. The Negroes of the *Tecora* had been landed and sold with the complicity of corrupt Havana authorities. On June 28 they were put aboard the *Amistad,* a coastal schooner, bound for Puerto Principe and the sugar plantations of western Cuba. The slave traders, Ruiz and Montez, accompanied their illicit property.

The grim jest of a crew member led the Africans to believe that they were to be massacred on arrival. On the fourth night out they broke through their chains, and the following morning, led by an African named Cinque, they rushed the captain and split his head open with a machete. They also killed the cook, who had made the threatening jest. Two of the remaining crew members escaped in a small boat and spread the alarm. The lives of the owners were spared on the promise to pilot the ship eastward to Africa. Ruiz and Montez kept the vessel pointed east by day, but at night they steered to the American coast, hoping to arrive in a Southern port. Because of the devious navigation, however, the *Amistad* took a northerly direction and turned up off Montauk Point, Long Island. There she was taken into custody by a United States coastal brig, the *Washington,* and then brought into New London, Connecticut.

The Cuban slave traders immediately denounced Cinque and his tribesmen as revolted slaves, pirates and murderers; Captain Gedney, the master of the *Washington,* put in a claim for salvage which included both the ship and her slave cargo. Upon hearing of the capture, the Spanish minister to Washington demanded that the prisoners be delivered up for justice in Havana. Secretary of State John Forsyth, a Georgia slaveholder, was quite willing to comply with the demand. The Negroes would have been shipped to certain death had it not been for the unthinking initiative of District Attorney Holabird, who had arraigned the Africans for murder before the United States Circuit Court in New Haven in a trial set

NEW HAVEN
COLONY
HISTORICAL SOCIETY

Cinque, kidnapped from his homeland, led the
slave revolt against the *Amistad* crew.

for September 19. Ironically, this action placed the Negroes
out of the reach of harm. To have superseded the authority of the court would have been a dangerous expedient
under any circumstances, and especially in view of the impending Presidential elections. Nevertheless, Van Buren
clearly indicated where his sympathies lay by ordering the
Grampus to New Haven to immediately transport the
Negroes to Havana if they were found guilty. If the decision
went against the prosecution, the district attorney was instructed to appeal forthwith to the Supreme Court. No preparations were made to transport the Africans to their
homeland if freed. Two governments, the President of the
United States, all the members of his cabinet, a majority of
Congress and the full force of the slave South were arrayed
against these miserable, uprooted, penniless men who could
not speak a word of English or any European language.

Their doom would have been inevitable if the abolitionists had not intervened. As soon as news of the case reached antislavery headquarters, steps were taken to aid the unfortunate Africans. The support of prominent citizens was solicited, funds were collected, publicity was issued to the press, a search was undertaken among African sailors to find an interpreter who spoke the Mendi dialect of the defendants, and a battery of attorneys was retained, headed by Roger Sherman Baldwin of New Haven, grandson of the revolutionary patriot. Finally John Quincy Adams was approached to advise the legal staff on the complicated points of international law involved and to place the weight of his prestige on the side of the defense. At first Adams was reluctant to become involved in a new battle, but his conscience would not let him stand aside. He wrote a lengthy opinion on the diplomatic aspects of the case. Although it was a private letter, his abolitionist correspondent leaked parts of it to the press to acquaint the public with the ex-President's stand. Adams also offered his legal services to the defense, but they were not accepted at that time.

The trial lasted a full week. In general, the people of New Haven were sympathetic to the captive Negroes and the courtroom was filled each day with local citizens. The defense attorney, Baldwin, based his case on the fact that the Africans were free men, not slaves. The fact that they had been kidnapped, smuggled out of their native land and then sold into slavery, in utter defiance of international law and covenants between nations, did not alter their condition as freemen. It was in defense of their liberty that they had rebelled so violently with such tragic consequences. A white man in their position, Baldwin argued, citing instances of Barbary Coast piracy, would never be treated as property, even though he was so regarded under the laws of Algiers. "The same rule," he insisted, "must apply to the black man as to the white man." The principal argument of the prosecution was a demand for respect of treaty obligations to Spain, which required the Negroes to be returned to the Spanish claimant.

The decision of Judge Judson was almost completely favorable to the defense. He awarded salvage money on the vessel and its material cargo to Captain Gedney and ordered Antonio, the cabin boy and a real slave (not one of the African group), to be turned over to the Spanish authorities for delivery to his owner. The other prisoners, he held, were free men, and he ordered them released in the custody of the President pending their return to Africa. The laws of Spain and of the United States were the warrant for his decision. The district attorney appealed the verdict at once and the Africans remained in custody.

That winter Adams sparked the issue in the House. He obliged the President to furnish Congress with all official documentation concerning the *Amistad* case. In these papers he seized upon a faulty translation of a Spanish term which appeared deliberately to distort a vital point in the case. A Congressional committee was appointed to investigate. Meanwhile he introduced resolutions deploring the continued imprisonment of the Africans, which he managed to read from the floor, although the House refused to receive them. The public was not allowed to forget the *Amistad* Case while the Supreme Court was in recess.

As the new trial drew near, the defense committee approached New England's most prominent lawyers to appear for the defendants. When Daniel Webster and Rufus Choate declined, they turned to John Quincy Adams. Two of the abolitionist leaders, Lewis Tappan and Ellis Grey Loring, went to the Adams home in Quincy to persuade him to accept.

The old man first resisted their entreaties: "I am too old, too oppressed by my duties in the House of Representatives, too inexperienced after a lapse of thirty years in the forms and technicalities of arguments before the Supreme Court. . . ."

His qualms were understandable, they agreed, but what of

the unfortunate Africans suspended between life and death?

Deeply moved, Adams acquiesced: "By the blessings of God I will argue the case before the Supreme Court."

Charles was disturbed by his father's new venture, which he believed might affect his own chances for election to the Massachusetts legislature. The electorate had no such misgivings: It gave him an easy victory and reelected his intrepid parent to Congress by a two-thirds majority.

John Quincy was seventy-four years old when he left for Washington that November. He believed that this would be his last term in Congress and his last great service to humanity. "My eyes are threatening to fail me," he recorded in his journal. "My hands tremble like an aspen leaf. My memory daily deserts me. My imagination is fallen into the sear and yellow leaf and my judgment sinking into dotage. . . ."

It was far from a senile old man who reviewed the case in great detail with Roger Baldwin in New Haven. He also visited the African prisoners and was impressed by the appearance of their two most prominent leaders, Cinque and Grabeau. When Adams arrived in Washington, letters were waiting for him from two of the Africans who had learned a rudimentary English during their long imprisonment.

"Dear Friend Mr. Adams," one of them read. ". . . What for Americans keep us in prison. Some people say Mendi people crazy dolts because we no talk American language. Americans no talk Mendi. American people crazy dolts. . . . Dear friend Mr. Adams you have children and friends you love them you feel very sorry if Mendi people come and take all to Africa. Cook say he kill, he eat Mendi people—we afraid—we kill cook. . . . We never kill captain if he no kill us. . . . All we want is make us free."

The Supreme Court opened its sessions on February 22, 1841, the anniversary of the birthday of George Washington, and of the signing of the Transatlantic Treaty with Spain. If these signs were favorable, the composition of the high tribunal was not; a majority of the justices were Southern slaveholders or "Northern men with Southern principles." The first day was occupied with arguments by Attorney General Henry D. Gilpin for the government and Roger Baldwin for the defense, and the session was concluded with Gilpin's rebuttal.

On the following day Adams rose to make the concluding argument for the defense. He had been nervous and apprehensive while making the most meticulous and exhaustive preparations for his plea; it had been thirty-seven years since his last appearance before this court. But as he warmed to his subject, the inimitable fighting form of Old Man Eloquent reasserted itself. For four hours he held the undivided attention of the judges and a crowded gallery.

He maintained that the Africans had been torn from their own country, transported against the laws of Spain, against the laws of the United States, against the law of nations. Then he poured his scorn upon the President and his Secretary of State. Instead of acting as constable for the Spaniards, the President, he declared, should have peremptorily rejected the offensive demands of the Spanish minister, who had objected to a trial on American soil. Not only had they degraded the country by their silence, but they had conspired with the slave smugglers and the man hunters.

"Was ever such a scene of liliputian trickery enacted by the rulers of a great, magnanimous, and Christian nation?" he demanded. "Contrast it with that act of self-emancipation by which the savage, heathen barbarians, Cinque and Grabeau, liberated themselves and their fellow suffering countrymen from the Spanish slave traders . . . Cinque and Grabeau are uncouth and barbarous names. Call them Harmodius and Aristogiton, and go back for moral principles three thousand years to the fierce and glorious democracy of Athens. They too resorted to lawless violence and slew the tyrant to redeem the freedom of their country. For this heroic action they paid the forfeit of their lives. But within three years the Athenians expelled their tyrants, and in gratitude to their deliverers decreed that henceforth no slave should bear either of their names. Cinque and Grabeau are not slaves. Let them bear in future history the names of Harmodius and Aristogiton!"

It was an extraordinary performance, Justice Story commented as the Court recessed. "Extraordinary for its power and its bitter sarcasm, and its dealing with topics beyond the record and points of discussion."

When the court reconvened on March 1, Adams continued his argument for another three hours. His concluding words were a moving, personal plea to the assembled justices. He reminded them that the last time he had appeared before this bench was in 1804; in the intervening years he had been summoned by the government to other duties. "Little did I imagine that I should ever again be required to claim the right of appearing in the capacity of officer of this Court; yet such has been the dictate of my destiny—and I appear again to plead the cause of justice, and now of liberty and life, in behalf of my fellow men, before that same Court, which in a former age I had addressed in support of rights of property. . . . I stand before the *same* Court, but not the same judges. . . . Marshall—Cushing—Chase—Washington—Johnson—Livingston—Todd—Where are they? Gone! All gone! Gone from the services . . . they faithfully rendered to their country. . . . In taking then my final leave from this Honorable Court, I can only ejaculate a fervent petition to heaven that every member of it may go to his final account with as little of earthly frailty to answer for as those illustrious dead. . . ."

After hearing concluding arguments from Baldwin and the Attorney General, the justices retired to deliberate. On March 9 they returned to render their decision. It was a complete victory for the defense. Only one judge dissented.

Adams was beside himself with joy. "The captives are free!" he wrote Lewis Tappan. "Not unto us! Not unto us! but thanks in the name of humanity and justice to *you!*"

Baldwin replied: "Glorious! Glorious not only as a triumph of humanity and justice, but as a vindication of our national character from reproach and dishonor." And from Whittier, an abolitionist leader who had quarreled with Adams over his stand on slavery in the District of Columbia, came the apology: ". . . I believe we now all appreciate thy motives and while we regret that there should be differences of opinion between us, we feel that thou art entitled to our warmest gratitude as abolitionists."

From Charles come a sigh of relief and a tepid message of congratulation.

You see, Adams replied to his son, it had been right to fight. Then he reminded him somewhat reproachfully that "the agony of soul that I suffered" during his involvement in the case "was chiefly occasioned by the reprobation of my own family, both of my opinions and my conduct, and their terror at the calamities which they anticipated they would bring upon *them.* . . ."

If the tone was harsh, the spirit of this lesson in moral courage that father had bequeathed to son was immortal.

17

The Gag Rule
Is Broken

WHEN ADAMS began his epic combat against slavery, he stood alone in Congress, a solitary figure opposed by the solid slaveholding South and their Northern allies. It was a crushing burden for a man of his advanced years. At one point he hoped for someone else "capable of taking the lead in the cause of universal emancipation" so that he could "withdraw from the contest which will rage with increasing fury as it draws to its crisis." Unfortunately, "there is no such man in the House."

The picture had greatly altered as the decade of the 1840's opened. A small but determined group of Northern Congressmen joined the battle for the right of petition. Joshua Giddings, the most prominent among them, commented: "There has been a great revolution going on here as to human rights since Mr. Adams began his 'flare up,' and many members now wish themselves to be regarded as the advocates of the rights of man who would have been angry at being called an abolitionist six months ago."

Adams's wish had been answered, but he had already forgotten his resolution to leave the field of battle when relief arrived. On the contrary, he plunged into the melee with greater zeal than ever. Only "physical force," he told the

House, would silence him. He wrote to a Pennsylvania Anti-Slavery Society that he had dedicated the remainder of his life to the overthrow of slavery. "When it shall be done peaceably or by blood," he added, "God only knows. But it shall be accomplished I have no doubt; and by whatever way, I say let it come."

Year after year Adams had hammered at the gag rule. It seemed nothing could dislodge the firmly entrenched practice, certainly not the efforts of one or even several men. But gradually cracks began to appear in the solid wall. The majorities favoring the curtailment of the right of petition began to dwindle. Northern Congressmen did not respond with the same alacrity to the crack of the slaveholder's political whip. The Whig party began to divide along sectional lines.

There had been a regular majority of 48 or 49 votes for the imposition of the gag rule at each session of Congress. But the number of members from free states voting for it began to diminish. In 1836, 82 out of 117 Northerners voted in favor of it. Three years later, there were only 49 out of 126. In 1840, the most rigorous of all the gags barely carried, with a majority of only 6 votes, and counting only 26 Northerners in the affirmative. At a special session in the summer of 1841, Adams again moved to rescind the gag rule, and on the first roll call his motion carried by 112 to 104; but on the final vote, the New Hampshire and Maine delegations broke ranks, and the motion lost by the narrow margin of 110 to 106. At the regular session that December, Adams renewed his attack and lost by two votes; only 21 Northerners now remained in the Southern camp.

The Whig coalition was in mortal danger. One more mighty effort would topple the walls of privilege, and bring the hosts of abolition within the gates. Congress would then cease to be an exclusive slaveholders' club; the great issues of freedom versus slavery would be freely ventilated; representatives would vote their convictions instead of their fears. The spearhead of the drive of Congressional freedom had to be blunted and smashed before it was too late. John Quincy Adams had to be broken, the Southerners resolved, before he broke them.

When Congress resumed its sessions in January 1841 Adams continued firing his salvos against slavery.

He presented six petitions in rapid succession. One urged the government to replace the despotic governments of slaveholding states by a "republican form of government"; another objected to a war against England for the preservation of slavery in the United States; another argued for the right of "free colored persons to become American citizens and to own real estate"; a fourth demanded that citizens conscientiously obey the provisions of the Constitution in taking up arms for the protection of slaveholders; a fifth from forty-one Negro seamen demanded redress from restrictions imposed on them in Southern ports.

No sooner was each petition read than Representative Wise was on the floor with a motion to table it. Each time the motion carried.

Then came a sixth petition from citizens of Georgia protesting Adams's appointment as chairman of the Committee on Foreign Affairs. Wise promptly objected to receiving the paper. Representative Habersham of Georgia declared the petition to be a hoax. Amidst the commotion, Adams demanded that the paper be read and that he be heard in his own defense.

The document was finally read. Its authors granted Adams all the necessary qualifications and patriotism for the office but believed him possessed with a "species of monomania on all subjects connected with people as dark as Mexicans, and therefore not fitted to be entrusted with the business of our relations with Mexico."

Southern members were divided on the question of whether Adams should be allowed to reply to the charges made in the petition. One Congressman maintained that Adams was entitled to the floor even though he was a "monomaniac." Another said the House was not competent to judge on lunacy. Finally, the petition was laid on the table but before the House adjourned the Speaker accorded Adams the right to reply.

When Adams attempted to speak the following morning, however, he was interrupted by points of order from Wise and others. The Speaker urged the old man to proceed. "Yes, Sir," Adams replied, raising his voice, "provided there are no fifty or one hundred questions of order raised to gag me—"

There was another uproar and Adams was directed to take his seat. Once more the House had to vote to allow him to continue. When Adams again had the floor he proceeded to denounce the alliance of Southern slave-traders and their Northern auxiliaries as responsible for the attempt to remove him and demanded it be dissolved. He then proposed to read a letter from Wise. The Speaker ruled him out of order, but on appeal the ruling was defeated 76 to 78.

"I shall now have the privilege of reading this delectable letter," Adams began with relish. It was a complaint by Wise against the appointment of a majority of nonslaveholders to a committee to discuss the recognition of Haiti. Such was the impartiality of a slaveholder, Adams commented.

Representative Rayner of North Carolina quickly moved to cut him off on the grounds that a discussion of slavery was not in order, and he requested the House "to arrest the course of the gentleman from Massachusetts who was disgracing himself and disgracing the country by playing the mountebank and the harlequin before the grand inquest of the nation."

"I see where the shoe pinches, Mr. Speaker," Adams growled, "it will pinch more yet . . . If before I get through every slaveholder, slave trader and slave breeder on this floor does not get materials for better reflection it shall be no fault of mine."

In the midst of angry words and repeated shouts of order, the House adjourned.

The following Monday, Wise succeeded in passing his motion to halt Adams's speech. By well-timed exposure, a plot to remove Adams from the chairmanship of the committee had been thwarted. The petition may have been a hoax, but the plot was real enough, for soon afterward five Southern members resigned from the committee, and of five other Southerners appointed in their place, three refused to serve under Adams.

Adams next presented a petition from forty-five citizens of Haverhill, Massachusetts, urging Congress immediately to adopt measures "peaceably to dissolve the Union of these States." He proposed the paper be referred to a select committee with a recommendation to report back the reasons for its rejection.

Still underestimating the old fox, the opposition gloated, thinking he had stepped right into their trap. It had been decided in a secret Whig caucus to urge Southern members to censure Adams, and now it seemed he himself had given them their opportunity.

"Is it in order to burn the petition in the presence of the House?" shouted Hopkins of Virginia.

"Is it in order to censure the member presenting the petition?" Wise inquired of the Speaker.

"Good!" Adams called from his seat.

When a Southern Representative objected to such petitions coming within the walls of the House, Adams expressed surprise that an objection should come from a part of the Union where nullification was far from unpopular.

A motion was made to adjourn, but Adams objected in view of the pending motion of censure, which had been introduced by Thomas Gilmer of Virginia.

Adams hoped that the censure motion would be debated and that he would be given the chance to defend himself, especially, he added with cutting sarcasm, as Gilmer thought it proper to play second fiddle to Wise.

At this remark a great roar went up.

Gilmer shouted to the Speaker: "I play second fiddle to no man. I am endeavoring to stop the music of one

'Who in the course of one revolving moon,
Was poet, fiddler, statesman, and buffoon.' "

Gilmer's motion was superseded by a more elaborate resolution presented by Thomas Marshall of Kentucky. Censuring an ex-President was, after all, a very serious matter, and it would have to be justified to the hilt. "Dissolution of the Union," the indictment read, "necessarily implies . . . the overthrow of the American Republic, and the extinction of our national existence." By presenting such a petition, Adams had "offered the deepest indignity to the House of which he is a member; an insult to the people of the United States. . . ." For this, the resolution concluded, he "might well be held to merit expulsion . . ." but "the House deem it an act of grace and mercy, when they only inflict upon him their severest censure for conduct so unworthy of his past relation to the State, and his present position . . . for the rest they turn him over to his own conscience and the indignation of all true *American* citizens."

This proposal was influenced less by "grace and mercy" than by the fact that Adams's detractors lacked the two-thirds majority required for expulsion.

Defending his resolution, Marshall declared that while he had the highest esteem for the gentleman from Massachusetts, the House could not tolerate the incitement to "high treason" contained in the Haverhill petition.

The galleries were crowded with hostile proslavery men when the old man rose to reply. His voice was high-pitched as usual, but clear, untremulous and firm. "What is high treason?" Adams asked in a tone of mock surprise. "The Constitution of the United States says what it is . . ." and turning to Marshall, his voice changed to withering scorn: "It is not for the puny mind of the gentleman of Kentucky to define what high treason is and confound it with what I have done."

"Read the first paragraph of the Declaration of Independence!" Adams ordered the clerk.

The clerk read: "When in the course of human events, it becomes necessary for one people to dissolve the political bands which have connected them with another, and to assume among the powers of the earth, the separate and equal station to which the Laws of Nature and of Nature's God entitle them. . . ."

"Read it! Read it!" came the command from the son of one of the originators of the Declaration. "Read it, down to the 'right and duty.' "

Slowly the clerk made his way to the vital section: "—Prudence, indeed, will dictate that Governments long established should not be changed for light and transient causes . . . But when a long chain of abuses and usurpations, pursuing invariably the same Object evinces a design to reduce them under absolute Despotism, it is their right, it is their duty, to throw off such Government, and to provide new Guards for their future security."

"Read that again!" Adams thundered. His slight, drooping frame seemed rejuvenated as his historic vindication was recited.

"I rest that petition on the Declaration of Independence," Adams resumed. He saw no reason yet for the people to invoke the "right of revolution." But if they were deprived of the right of petition, among other liberties, they would have no other recourse. It was within the powers of Congress, he concluded, to convince the people that Constitutional means for the redress of their grievances were still available. A first step would be to receive and answer the Haverhill petition.

The impatient conspirators demanded that Adams conclude his defense forthwith, refusing his request for adequate time to make preparations. Fortunately Wise's immediate rebuttal occupied the House for two days, and Adams used the time to prepare the notes for his defense.

Wise began his remarks with an attempted parody of

Adams's speech. He called on the clerk to read Washington's Farewell Address, and when the clerk came to a famous passage, he shouted, "Read that again!" It was in such bad taste and so absurd that the laughter of the audience turned against the speaker himself. At least some of his listeners snorted in derision at Wise's preposterous warning: "Break down slavery, and you would with one blow destroy the great democratic principle of equality among men." John Quincy Adams, he intoned, had outlived his time and his fame. He no longer had sufficient influence "to excite a spirit of disunion throughout the land. . . . The gentleman is politically dead, dead as Burr—dead as Arnold. The people would look upon him with wonder, will shudder, and retire."

Old Man Eloquent was far from dead, politically or otherwise, as Wise soon discovered. "He is like one of those old cardinals," Ralph Waldo Emerson commented, scoffing at this funereal talk, "who quick as he is chosen Pope, throws away his crutches and crookedness, and is straight as a boy." Louisa Adams marveled at "the beautiful composure of his mind," at "the facility with which he selects documents and bygone facts suitable for his purposes . . . and always thoroughly applicable . . . almost incredible for a man of his years." In the midst of it all, she complained, he received visitors and read the many letters addressed to him.

The eyes of the nation were upon Adams as he rose in the House to reply to his accusers. He had no apologies to make, no words to retract, and he asked for no mercy. Let those who had insulted, reviled and slandered him punish him if they dared. "I defy them to expel me. I have constituents to go to who will have something to say if this House expels me. Nor will it be long before gentlemen will see me here again!"

His first target was the swashbuckling Wise. What right had this man, who had been deeply implicated in the death of Jonathan Cilley in the Cilley-Graves duel, to speak of treason or sit in judgment over John Quincy Adams? Graves had fired the fatal bullet, but "that far more guilty man," Adams cried out, "came into this House with his hands and face dripping—when the blood spots were yet visible upon him. . . . It is very possible that I saved this blood-stained man from the censure of the House . . . although his hands were reeking with the blood of murder."

Wise went pale. He "writhed and gasped for a few moments," wrote a New York reporter, "and then sprang up convulsively, and stretched out a quivering hand as if he thought to clutch the throat of his enemy, burst out in a voice between a scream and a hoarse whisper and imploringly protested his innocence. . . ."

Marshall's turn was next. Toward the Kentuckian, young enough to be his son, Adams adopted a more patronizing tone. The young man had a future if he could overcome his vices, he advised. Adams was perplexed that the nephew of the late Chief Justice of the Supreme Court should know so little of the law. "Let him go home," the old man urged paternally, "and attend some law school and learn a little of the rights of the citizens of these states and the members of this House."

Then Adams turned to Gilmer. In his hand was another threatening letter, sent from Norfolk, Virginia, which seemed to have been directly inspired by Gilmer. "Stop the music of John Quincy Adams, sixth President of the United States," it began. Then with slight alteration followed the verse Gilmer had quoted. And it concluded: "Unless you very soon change your course, death will be your portion. Prepare, prepare . . . you will be unexpectedly hurled into Eternity where you ought to have been long since." Such were the allies of the man who wanted to bring down upon him the censure of the House, Adams remarked scornfully.

This House, Adams charged, could not be an impartial court because there were one hundred members in it who had a personal and pecuniary interest in slavery. His voice swelled with pride: "I come from a portion of the country where slavery is only known by name . . . from a soil that bears not the foot of a slave upon it. . . ."

Observers feared that violence would erupt at Adams's

fiery tirade. Some Southern members were armed, and the House seemed on the verge of a riot. But the tide was turning. Under Adams's remorseless pounding day after day the solid front began to break. Underwood of Kentucky warned his Southern colleagues to "beware how they put it in the hands of the gentleman from Massachusetts to go home and tell his constituents that he was a martyr to the right of petition."

He was followed by Botts of Virginia, who said Adams had not been the first to introduce the subject of dissolution in the House. A Southerner had had that distinction. Moreover, he continued, the Secretary of the Navy "is an open, avowed, undisguised advocate of the immediate dissolution of the Union."

"I deny it," interjected Wise.

"What authority do you have?" Botts flung back. "Do you keep a record of the conversations of the Secretary of the Navy?"

The enemy was wrangling among themselves—a sure sign of their impending rout.

"Old Seventy-Six," a reporter wrote, "still keeps his ground like a hero. . . . A large portion of the Southern Whigs . . . see that the North is rallying in overwhelming force to the venerable champion of Northern liberty and equal rights . . . They know that they must make terms with us. . . ."

Gilmer was the first to offer a truce; he would withdraw his motion of censure if Adams would withdraw his petition. Adams vehemently refused. "No! No! I cannot do that. . . . If I withdraw the petition I would consider myself as having sacrificed the right of petition . . . the right of habeas corpus . . . the right of trial by jury . . . sacrificed the sacred confidence of the post office . . . freedom of the press . . . freedom of speech. . . . If the representatives should be intimidated from the discharge of their duty, they, the people, would be their own champions and the defenders of their own rights. *There* is the deadly character of the attempt to put me down."

Adams returned that evening, Louisa wrote her son in Boston, "greatly exhausted by his exertion, and literally tremulous from head to foot from fatigue." But the next morning he "arose with renewed vigor to pursue his duties in the House. . . ." To pursue his quarry might have been more precise.

From Gilmer he wrung the admission that he had been at a Southern caucus before the censure motion and there had proposed to replace Adams as chairman of the Foreign Affairs Committee. In the end, before the hoax had failed, it had been decided to give the post to a pliable New Englander. Who, demanded Adams, was out of his wits now? Silence was the only reply.

Marshall had disclaimed any sympathy with Wise's speech, but he delivered a tirade against Adams, denying that he had charged him with treason but insisting that Adams was guilty of contempt. The old man replied by reading a famous letter Marshall had written a year before, which had been published in Kentucky, denouncing slavery and urging an immediate remedy.

Point by point, man by man, Adams silenced his critics. The North was aroused as it had rarely been before. A new flood of petitions inundated Congress demanding the cessation of the censure proceedings. Newspapers lashed the slaveholders' plot. An angry people had already defeated the censure motion, and when Adams rose on February 7, 1842, and told the House he required another week to complete his defense, the white flag went up. Botts made a motion to table the entire matter, including all the censure motions, and it passed by a vote of 106 to 93.

"Right Vindicated and Victorious!" wrote the *New York American* correspondent. "Few, very few men of any age would have stood up with such indomitable firmness, such ability, such eloquence as he [Adams] has evinced in resistance of the wrong meditated against Liberty!"

The old man had won the unstinted gratitude of the North. A great abolitionist meeting in Faneuil Hall, for the first time unmolested by pro-slavery mobs, adopted a resolution praising John Quincy Adams for his "bold, faithful and indefatigable advocacy of the right of petition under circumstances of great difficulty and peril." The Erie County Anti-Slavery Society declared that "in the midst of bullies and bowie knives . . . for the thousandth time has that great and good man covered his silvered head with imperishable glory." The citizens of Port Byron congratulated "John Quincy Adams in his manful defense of the sacred right of petition against the combined influence of the slaveocracy. . . ." With this battle, Adams had finally won his family to his side. "To be his wife and your mother," Louisa wrote to Charles in a letter John Quincy did not see, "is all the dignity I can crave on this side of the bourne to which we hourly bend our way. . . ."

For a moment the South was cowed, and when Representative Barnard of Rochester, New York, presented a petition calling for dissolution in terms similar to the famous Haverhill document, it was merely tabled by the House without any fuss. The calm was short-lived, however, and the South soon renewed its efforts to silence the antislavery forces. Joshua Giddings of Ohio had introduced a resolution opposing demands of slaveholders for compensation for the liberated slaves of the *Creole,* an American vessel which had been captured by the bondsmen and brought into a British port in the Bahamas. Giddings was summarily censured and denied the opportunity to speak in his own behalf. The Congressman resigned his seat and returned to his district in the Western Reserve, where he was reelected on a straightforward antislavery platform by a landslide majority.

Giddings' reelection consolidated Adams's victory and constituted a turning point in the struggle. Back in Congress, Giddings was threatened with another censure resolution if he introduced a new motion on the *Creole* affair. It was an empty threat, for no censure attempt was made when Giddings presented his motion. Slavery was becoming a subject for open discussion in the House.

"Abolitionism is talked not only at our table, but all over Washington," the antislavery leader Theodore Weld wrote his wife. "The truth is," he continued, "that the slaveholders got so smitten with consternation with the bolts father Adams hurled through their ranks last session, that they have never been able to rally."

Adams made the most of the favorable winds that now filled his sails. Together with other Whig antislavery insurgents he signed an appeal to the nation calling upon the people to break the gag rule with a mighty cataract of petitions. There had been a time when the people were begging for Congressmen to present their petitions; now Congressmen were begging the people to submit them. The following year Charles Francis Adams secured the passage of a resolution by the Massachusetts legislature calling upon Congress to enact a Constitutional amendment to abolish the three-fifths rule—the slavery bonus—of determining representation in the House of Representatives. John Quincy Adams was proud to present his son's resolution in Congress. After a long debate, the resolution was referred to a committee whose majority membership was opposed to the amendment. The unfavorable committee report was adopted by the House, but Adams refused to be defeated. Three times in 1844 he reintroduced the resolution. That it was defeated was less important, Adams calculated, than that it should be talked about; it would educate the people in the undemocratic nature of the slaveholder's strength in Congress.

This battle was just beginning when an old one ended in victory. On December 3, 1844, the opening of the Twenty-eighth Congress, Adams introduced his customary resolution to rescind the gag rule. *The resolution was carried by a vote of 105 to 80.* Adams had reconquered the right of petition for the American people. The slave power was still a formidable force, but it had lost its stranglehold on Congress and its opponents could now voice their opinions in fair debate. Through the voices of courageous men the slave would have a forum for his terrible grievances.

18

War with Mexico

IN THE BACKGROUND of the censure controversy was the issue of Texas. Northern opposition forced the annexationists to operate undercover and to rely principally on secrecy and surprise. But the thousands of petitions against annexation, championed by an ex-President, forced them into the open when they desired it least. Adams, a veteran diplomat, anticipated their maneuvers, predicted their moves, tied their hands by constant exposure. He was the eyes and ears of the antislavery North. Had he been muzzled, the North might have been cowed into silence and then confronted one day, without warning, with the accomplished fact of annexation. But the plot failed and for a time the "slaveocracy," as Adams called it, was stymied.

Hardly a month had passed since the attempt to censure Adams when the battle over Texas flared up again in Congress. It was precipitated by President Tyler's nomination of Waddy Thompson of South Carolina as ambassador to Mexico. It was Thompson who had once threatened Adams with the grand jury and whom Adams described as "the most inveterate enemy of Mexico during his whole career in Congress." John Tyler had assumed the Presidency upon the death of William Henry Harrison, a Northern Whig, who died a few months after his inauguration in 1841. He was a Virginia slaveholder and an ardent pro-annexationist, as were most of the members of his cabinet. Antislavery Congressmen were worried by his truculent, aggressive attitude toward Mexico over disputes they believed were negotiable. Adams thought the administration was trying to pick a quarrel that would lead to a war whose real object was the conquest of Texas.

The situation was further complicated by strained relations with England over unresolved boundaries in the Northeast and in the Oregon country and over America's dilatory enforcement of treaties outlawing the slave trade. The two nations were also at loggerheads over Texas. Britain wanted the territory to remain independent to serve as a free-labor competitor with the South and as a means of stabilizing peaceful relations with Mexico.

Henry Wise seized the opportunity offered by the debate on Thompson's nomination to deliver an openly bellicose speech. There were good reasons, he held, to justify a war with Mexico. One was the collection of claims which the United States had been awarded by the arbitration commission some years ago but which Mexico had not yet paid. Another was to avenge the mistreatment of American citizens who had been captured in an expedition against Santa Fe on Mexican territory. His final argument was the defense of slavery against Santa Anna's recent threat to "drive slavery beyond the Sabine River."

Thousands of volunteers from the great Mississippi Valley were waiting for the call to arms, Wise declared. They would conquer Mexico and bring the church-ridden government to its knees. Not only Texas, but the entire Southwest as far as the Pacific Ocean would then be open to slavery. He for one had no fear of England. "Let a war come, with France, the United States and Texas on one side, and England and Mexico on the other. I would ask for nothing better."

Wise was followed by Ingersoll of Pennsylvania, who was not to be outdone in warlike fervor. The nation, he boasted, was in a high state of war preparations and would stand for no nonsense from England. It was monstrous humbug to talk of the British navy going to New York and burning it. He had been told by the first officer of the American navy that if they burned New York we would burn London, five times as big, and this officer himself would answer for it! The House roared with laughter at this preposterous boast.

When the laughter subsided, John Quincy Adams rose to reply. Pointing to the windows he said, as if agreeing with Ingersoll, "No, we are not unprepared at all—because we have in the sight of the windows of the Capitol two armed steamers; one of them I am informed nearly disabled, so that she will need in a great measure to be rebuilt. So that in case of immediate hostilities, we have one entire steamer, and with that we are to burn London. . . . The gentleman did admit that it was very probable that New York should be burnt too, yet as London was four or five times as large, we should have the balance of burning on our side."

Once again the House roared. The only thing that burned that day were the cheeks of the Pennsylvania Congressman.

Adams continued in a more serious vein. A war for the causes set forth by Wise would not be a just war. Claims, he asserted, should not be settled by war, the most irresponsible and costly way of collecting debts. The American citizens who were prisoners in Mexico had been caught red-handed on foreign soil in an act of war in which the United States government had no part; sweeping the streets of Mexican cities was indeed a moderate penalty compared to that which Jackson had meted out to Ambrister and Arbuthnot. And if the United States were to go to war to save slavery in Texas, "Then let it be proclaimed from the housetops—the sooner my constituents know it, the better!" Adams held no brief for General Santa Anna, who might be, he readily conceded, a merciless tyrant. But he would never support a war over differences which could be settled by a minimum of good will. "Military men," he declared, "are bound to take it for granted that their country is in the right, when those departments of the government to whom the right of judging is consigned have so determined. The question of right and wrong is a question for such an assembly as this to decide, and not for the deck of a man-of-war. . . ."

Once again he cited his own role in the history of Texas. It was true, he agreed, that as President he had attempted to purchase Texas from Mexico. But it was at a time when slavery had been abolished from the territory by the parent government, and Texas, under those circumstances, would have entered the Union as a free state. He had not changed that position. The restoration of slavery, he reiterated, was the insurmountable reason "why I will never consent to the annexation of Texas . . . not if the territory were ten times more valuable than it is."

"So, I suppose," Adams concluded, "if war shall come, we shall not only acquire this solitary brilliant star of Texas, but we shall have all Mexico added to the United States . . . The gentleman [Wise] in his dreams told us that President Houston was to plant the lonely star on the walls of the city of Mexico, and that if he did not do it, the gentleman himself would [loud laughter]. And he means in this heroic enterprise to lead on the brave spirits of thousands from the great valley of the Mississippi, robbing priests and pillaging churches. . . . What is then to become of the liberties of these United States? Our liberties will stand as little chance . . . as those of the nine millions of Mexico after he shall have conquered them. . . . And I look forward when, in the records of history, the gentleman's name shall be placed side by side, not with the names of Genghis Khan or Tamerlane, but with that of a still more glorious conqueror by the name of *Tom Thumb*."

Waves of laughter swept the hall as Adams resumed his seat.

Adams's speech had its intended effect. The Tyler administration resumed negotiations with Mexico. Their talks resulted in the release of the American prisoners and a new treaty for the payment of the outstanding claims awarded to the United States by the arbitration commission.

Once again Old Man Eloquent had averted a war with Mexico for the annexation of Texas. But this was to be the last time.

The following summer Adams took one of his rare vacations from politics. He joined his daughter-in-law, Mrs. Charles Francis Adams, her father, Peter Chardon Brooks, and his eldest grandson on a sight-seeing trip to Canada and Niagara Falls. The vacation turned unexpectedly into a triumphal tour. They traveled by rail across Massachusetts to Saratoga Springs, New York. There they boarded a stagecoach for an excursion around Lake George and Lake Champlain. They continued northward by steamer up the lakes and rivers and then again by stage to Montreal and Quebec.

They returned to the United States by way of Buffalo, where the red carpet of welcome was laid out for the old warrior. Thousands of persons thundered their greetings in a brief meeting in the city park and then lined the road waving and cheering as Adams and his official hosts proceeded in an open coach to his hotel. All along his homeward route he was welcomed with receptions, processions, and smiling, cheering, waving throngs. At a respectful distance, Americans had admired the man when he was their foremost diplomat and then their President, although they were far from unanimous in their sentiments toward him. But it was to Congressman Adams, who had fought against terrible odds for the lowliest of men, that the people opened their hearts.

This was only the beginning of the popular acclaim that awaited John Quincy Adams. In October he went to Cincinnati, where he had been invited to lecture on astronomy. Old

and ailing, Adams had accepted the invitation as an opportunity to win public support for his project of allocating the
Smithson bequest for a national observatory. It was a strenuous trip for a seventy-six-year-old man. A fierce snowstorm
delayed the steamer that took Adams across Lake Erie. The
next conveyance was a canal boat that inched along at two
and a half miles an hour. Passengers and crew were crammed
into a narrow space next to the stable for the tow horses.
Sleeping accommodations were settees on which the men
stretched out feet to feet. Fever and cough wracked the old
man's body.

When the lake steamer put into Erie, Pennsylvania, a military escort accompanied Adams to town. That night the fire-
men marched in a torchlight parade. In Cleveland, someone
recognized Adams in a barber shop, and an impromptu reception was hastily organized. At Akron, the public lined up
to shake the old man's hand; but a pretty young woman
kissed him on the cheek. Adams gingerly reciprocated and
then repeated the performance with relish with all the other
women in the queue. In Columbus, he was greeted by the
governor and spoke on astronomy at a public meeting. Accompanied by two military companies and a brass band, his
stagecoach was escorted across the Scioto River. There were
more crowds at Jefferson and Springfield, and at Dayton
there was a welcome in the grand style, Adams addressing
the multitude from his open carriage.

Cannon boomed as Adams approached Cincinnati. An official delegation headed by the mayor came out to meet him.
Great cheers went up from an enormous crowd as the mayor
made a formal speech of greeting. The following morning,
despite a pouring rain, another procession accompanied
Adams to the site for a local observatory, where he laid the
cornerstone. "JOHN QUINCY ADAMS, THE DEFENDER OF THE
RIGHTS OF MAN" read a banner strung across the street
through which the procession passed. That night, after concluding an address to an audience of two thousand persons

at a local theater, Adams was escorted back to his hotel through a double line of torchlights. The following evening a large audience listened with undivided attention to Adams's two-hour discourse on the history of astronomy.

There were invitations from Louisville and Lexington, Kentucky, from Indiana and from as far west as St. Louis. Adams regretfully declined them. But he did make a brief excursion to Covington and Maysville, Kentucky, where he was met by bands and processions. He was given a hero's welcome wherever the train stopped along the route of the Baltimore and Ohio to Washington. A full month after he had left Quincy, Adams arrived at his home in Washington. The journey had sapped almost his last ounce of strength, but never had his spirits been so high. The enthusiasm and affection that had greeted him everywhere were the supreme vindication for his lonely crusade in a just but unpopular cause.

Meanwhile Texas had once more become a political and diplomatic issue. Several European nations had accorded diplomatic recognition to the Lone Star Republic; Britain was attempting to secure recognition by Mexico in return for the abolition of slavery in Texas. Watching the drift of events from his retirement, Andrew Jackson impatiently prodded Tyler to act. We must have Texas, he wrote, "peaceably if we can, forcibly if we must." The pace quickened when Calhoun, a proslavery leader, became Secretary of State. On April 12, 1844, he signed a treaty of annexation with Sam Houston and sent it to the Senate for ratification. Its passage seemed certain until Calhoun committed the enormous blunder of informing the British ambassador at Washington that the United States had signed the treaty to prevent the abolition of slavery in Texas and thus to safeguard the institution in the Southern states. This was a totally unacceptable reason for annexation, and the Senate promptly rejected the treaty. Annexation quickly became an issue in the Presidential campaign. James Polk, the Democratic candidate, openly supported annexation, while Henry Clay, his Whig opponent, took a more equivocal position, and a third candidate, James Birney of the Liberty Party, was straightforward in his opposition.

John Quincy Adams was running for reelection to Congress. At a meeting presided over by his son at the Young Men's Whig Club in Boston he issued a fervent appeal for resistance.

"Your trial is approaching," he cried. "The spirit of freedom and the spirit of slavery are drawing together for the deadly conflict of arms. The annexation of Texas to this Union is the blast of the trumpet for a foreign, civil, servile, and Indian war, to which the government of your country, fallen into faithless hands, have already twice given the signal. . . . Young men of Boston: burnish your armor, prepare for the conflict, and I say to you in the language of Galgacus to the ancient Britons, think of your forefathers! Think of your posterity!"

His speech was printed and distributed throughout the country. The Whigs carried Massachusetts by a landslide and reelected Adams over two opponents. But Polk carried the country by a small plurality of popular votes as a result of the divided opposition.

Taking Polk's election as a mandate for annexation, Tyler resubmitted the Texas treaty to Congress when it reconvened late in December. It was submitted as a joint resolution to both houses, because the administration doubted it could command a two-thirds vote in the Senate, to whom treaties are usually submitted for ratification. Adams made a last effort to stave off annexation. Once again he recapitulated all the reasons for his opposition in a speech to the House on January 24, 1845. Only on one condition would he alter this opinion: "I am still willing to take Texas without slavery, *and with the assent of Mexico*. . . . Under those conditions I would go for Texas tomorrow."

The treaty was adopted and signed by John Tyler three

days before his term of office expired. "A signal triumph of the slave representation . . . the heaviest calamity that ever befell myself and my country was this day consummated," was Adams's bitter comment. He expected wars of conquest to follow in rapid succession that would lead to the dissolution of the Union.

Adams's prediction of war with Mexico was soon confirmed. After having given warning that it would consider annexation an act of war, Mexico withdrew its ambassador when the treaty with Texas was signed. President Polk countered by sending troops into Texas and arraying the United States fleet in the Gulf of Mexico and off the coast of California, also Mexican territory. He then sent John Slidell to Mexico with an offer to forfeit American claims in exchange for recognition of the Rio Grande boundary and the option to purchase all of New Mexico and California. When Mexico refused to receive Slidell, Polk ordered General Zachary Taylor to disputed border territory below the Rio Grande. In short order there was a clash with Mexican troops, and on April 23, 1846, President Paredes of Mexico declared a "defensive war." On May 11, President Polk sent a message to Congress stating that the two nations were at war because Mexico had invaded United States territory and proclaimed the beginning of hostilities. Four days later Congress voted a resolution declaring that "a state of war existed between the United States and Mexico" and authorized the President to take whatever measures were necessary to win it. The vote in the House was 174 to 14. John Quincy Adams voted against the resolution.

Adams wrote to Albert Gallatin that he could not support the war because it had always been our constant design to dismember Mexico, and he had always opposed that design. Taylor's advance into Mexico, he held, was an act of war taken without the consent of Congress, which set the dangerous precedent of taking the war powers from Congress and giving them to the President. The war, he contended,

United States troops and Mexican soldiers waged hand-to-hand combat in the Battle of Cerro Gordo.

was both unnecessary and unconstitutional. This was also the position of a fledgling Congressman from Illinois when he entered the House for the first time the following year. His name was Abraham Lincoln.

"It is not difficult to foresee what the ultimate issue will be to the people of Mexico," Adams concluded sadly, "but what it will be to the people of the United States, is beyond my foresight, and I turn my eyes away from it." Without knowing it, he was averting his eyes from the Civil War he would not live to see.

Since war was an accomplished fact, Adams voted for military appropriations to carry it on. He also voted for resolutions calling for its speedy termination without indemnity and without annexation.

At one time it had seemed to Adams that Northern opposition was so strong that no President would dare involve the country in a war with Mexico over Texas. When war actually came, the opposition dwindled to a small minority, determined and vocal, but still a minority. There were two important reasons for this reversal of Northern opinion. One was the widespread purchase of Texas bonds, which had declined sharply in value and which only annexation would restore to their original price. The second was the mood of expansionism which dominated the thinking of the people and to which Adams himself had so strongly contributed. If it was right to push the French out of Louisiana, the Spanish out of Florida and the English out of Oregon, why was it wrong to push the Mexicans out of Texas and California? There was, of course, a vast difference between a Mexican neighbor and European imperialist powers, but the people were momentarily blind to it. The people wanted land and more land, and the opportunities possession offered. As for slavery, they would attend to that later: the Southern plantation owners would not seize the new territories without a battle.

The war was only a few months old when that conflict

began. In response to President Polk's request for an appropriation of $2,000,000 from Congress to "facilitate negotiations," David Wilmot of Pennsylvania introduced an amendment prohibiting slavery in all new territories purchased by the treaty. It became known as the Wilmot Proviso, and in one or another form it was the central issue between North and South until the fatal shots were fired at Fort Sumter. Adams voted for the money bill when the proviso passed for the first and only time. He voted against the bill when the proviso had been defeated.

The old man made no speeches. Feeble, weary, he was almost eighty years old. "Proceed—Persevere—never despair—don't give up the ship!" he wrote to son Charles, who now stood shoulder to shoulder with his father in the antislavery cause.

19

The President Who
Became a Great Man

ON A SWELTERING MORNING in July, 1846, a young man swimming with his friends in the Potomac spied a familiar figure. "There is John Quincy Adams," he said. Out on his early morning stroll, the old man had been drawn by an "irresistible impulse" to the inviting water of the river. Finding his favorite rock taken, he left his clothes on another rock and was soon swimming as he had done often in the past. His dwindling strength, however, soon forced him to forego the sport he so enjoyed.

Back in Quincy with Louisa in August, he was invited to preside at a rally called in protest against the surrender of a fugitive slave. Five thousand persons in Faneuil Hall cheered John Quincy Adams as he walked down the aisle to the speaker's platform. He compared the meeting to one he had spoken at in the same hall thirty-eight years before in protest against the impressment of American seamen. The audience could see Adams, but the voice of Old Man Eloquent was almost inaudible, so only the few closest to him could hear his words.

When the Whig committee tendered him the unanimous nomination for Congress that autumn, he explained that he had voted against "the most unrighteous war" with Mexico.

They had no objection, and neither did the electors. He was reelected by a majority of 1,600 votes.

A few weeks later, he collapsed while out on a morning walk. His doctor diagnosed the cause as a light cerebral stroke, and for some days the old man seemed almost totally paralyzed. Later on he wrote in his diary: "From that hour I date my decease and consider myself, for every useful purpose to myself or to my fellow-creatures, dead."

But Adams was still very much alive. By the end of January 1847, he had resumed his stroll in the Boston streets, and on February 12, 1847, he was back in Washington accompanied by Louisa and his son Charles. The following morning, he entered the halls of Congress for the first time since his illness. The proceedings stopped, and every man rose from his seat to greet the venerable Congressman from Massachusetts. He was escorted to his seat by two of his colleagues in the midst of a standing, applauding House. How distant seemed the days of the gags, the insults, the epithets! The prophet was at last with honor in his own country.

Adams attended the session of Congress, but relinquished his membership on all but the Library of Congress Committee. He voted for a defeated resolution calling for the withdrawal of American troops to the eastern bank of the Rio Grande and for the conclusion of a peace without indemnities or territorial cessions. He spoke against a resolution to award $50,000 in damages to the owners of the *Amistad*. The resolution was overwhelmingly defeated.

That summer he returned to Quincy, but the following November he and Louisa were back in Washington. Once more he returned to his seat in Congress. By the winter of 1847 and 1848 it was clear the United States had the upper hand in the Mexican war, and a cry for the conquest of all Mexico began to be heard, just as Adams had once predicted. To restrain such a move, the President was asked to furnish Congress with all his diplomatic correspondence and his instructions to his officers concerning the return of Santa Anna to Mexico with American assistance. When President Polk refused to make certain letters available Adams asked for the floor.

"I think," he stated in a scarcely audible voice, "this House ought to sustain in the strongest manner, their right to call for information upon questions in which war and peace are concerned. . . . I should say more, sir, if I had the power."

On the afternoon of Friday, February 18, Adams prepared a report for his Congressional committee on the exchange of duplicate books among the libraries of Europe and the United States. That evening, he and Louisa held open house for a throng of visitors.

On Monday, February 21, Adams was in his place in the hall of the House. A vote was being taken on a motion to suspend the rules to consider a resolution of appreciation for the deeds of American generals in Mexico. In a firm and distinct voice Adams voted *No!* He had opposed the war as unjust; he could not now vote thanks to the generals who were waging it.

The motion itself was now ready to be submitted to a vote. The clerk read the resolution. Adams clutched the side of his desk, as if he wanted to rise from his seat and ask the right to be heard. Instead, he slumped back into his seat.

"Mr. Adams is dying!" one member cried out.

The business of the House stopped, and so did that of the Senate and the Supreme Court when the news reached them.

Carried into the Speaker's room, the dying man was laid on a sofa, where he was heard to say: "This is the last of earth—I am content." These were the last words of John Quincy Adams. For two days he lay in a deep coma, and on the evening of February 23, 1848, he passed away.

On the following day, both chambers of Congress convened to pay their final respect to their illustrious colleague. The great hall of the House was shrouded in black. Every seat was occupied—but one. Old Man Eloquent would never rise from that place again to fight for the rights of man. But only his physical presence was gone. His heroic combat for the liberation of men from human bondage had become a vivid chapter in the history and legends of Congress.

The Speaker of the House, Robert C. Winthrop of Massachusetts, pronounced a moving tribute:

"A seat on this floor has been vacated, towards which all eyes have been accustomed to turn with uncommon interest.

"A voice has been hushed forever, to which all ears have been wont to listen with profound reverence.

"He has been privileged to die at his post; to fall while in the discharge of his duties; and expire beneath the roof of the Capitol."

If these words ignored the years of struggle, they were also a posthumous triumph for John Quincy Adams.

By unanimous vote, the House voted that the seat of the member from Plymouth remain unoccupied and draped in black for thirty days, and that one member from each state and territory be designated to accompany the body to its final resting place.

The last rites for the departed statesman, President and soldier of liberty were a magnificent homage to one of the nation's leaders. Following the ceremonies in Washington, a black-draped funeral train carried the body of John Quincy Adams north to Quincy. Flags along the route were at half mast, and people bowed their heads as the train passed. Amidst the tolling of bells, Boston's citizens accompanied the catafalque to Faneuil Hall, where the body lay in state. Over the entrance of the hall was a placard on which were inscribed Adams's last words. Underneath it read: "John Quincy Adams. Born a citizen of Massachusetts. Died a citizen of the United States." In his funeral oration, Mayor Josiah Quincy of Boston said: "Tomorrow he will be 'gathered to his fathers,' and how great is the significance of that expression! . . . When again shall the tomb of a President of the United States open its doors to receive a son that has filled that same office?"

All business halted in the House of Representatives when John Quincy Adams collapsed at his desk.

A town meeting in Quincy met to offer its last homage to its greatest citizen, "to the truthful expositor of the principles upon which our republican institutions are based, a champion of the universal rights of man, and a promulgator of those ideas of human freedom shadowed forth in the Declaration of Independence and destined yet for a long time to agitate the world, till the rights of man, as man, are everywhere fully and practically acknowledged."

The bells tolled, and the cannon fired their final salute from the top of Penn's Hill, where young John and Abigail Adams had watched the flash of guns from the Battle of Bunker Hill across the bay.

The nation's leaders paid tribute to John Quincy Adams in a flood of eulogies. Most of them dwelt on his long life of service to the nation, his integrity, his unmatched qualities as a statesman. There they stopped, as though Adams had died when he left the Presidency or after his first few years in Congress; as though the memorable combat for freedom of speech and for "universal emancipation" had never been. It was like an unfinished tale, a biography whose last and perhaps most important chapter had been omitted. Nowhere was this more striking than in the arresting words of Thomas Hart Benton, Senator from Missouri, an opponent of Adams until the Texas question found them united. "Where," he asked, "could death have found him but at the post of duty?"

"Post of duty"—*on the field of battle in the war against slavery*. If the last phrase remained unspoken, it was because the war, in which Adams had fought the first skirmishes, was itself uncompleted; and in those early hours some men still refused to recognize its existence, others hoped that silence would make it vanish, others that a timely compromise would arrest its progress before it was too late. To have properly assessed Adams's role in history, one had to recognize that "the mighty years have begun"—to use the Biblical expression he had quoted to a friend some eight months before his death—and to accept the view that it was "the future destiny of our country to accomplish the glorious prophecy in the improvement of the condition of Man and in the abolition of slavery throughout the whole human race."

Only a man who had made a commitment to that "prophecy" could pronounce a fitting tribute to Old Man Eloquent, and it came from Theodore Parker, the famous abolitionist minister:

"The slave has lost a champion who gained new ardor and strength the longer he fought; America has lost a man who loved her with his heart; religion has lost a supporter; Freedom an unfailing friend, and mankind a noble vindicator of our inalienable rights."

The life of John Quincy Adams spanned eighty years. More than fifty of these were spent in the public service. Yet his most significant contribution to history was made in the last dozen years of a long and distinguished career. These last years were so radically different from all that had gone before as to give the impression of two separate and distinct lives. Was there in fact no link between the two lives, or was there something in the character and deeds of the man in the first phase that could have foretold the second and climactic phase?

Adams was born to the "purple," a hereditary member, so to speak, of the first "Establishment." His father was one of the galaxy of Revolutionary statesmen, a close associate of Washington, Jefferson, Hamilton, Madison and others. The elder Adams was also an outstanding leader of the conservative wing of the new Revolutionary government. After a brief hesitation, John Quincy embraced his father's views and joined him on the side of Edmund Burke against Thomas Paine. He was unsympathetic to the French Revolution because of its pronounced equalitarian tendencies. An opponent of monarchy, a staunch supporter of the rights of man under constitutional law, he nevertheless believed like his father in the rule of the elite. As a diplomat and President his policy was consistently conservative. In the White

House, he was the symbol of the *status quo* to the onrushing Jacksonion revolution.

Why did this pillar of respectability champion a radical and unpopular cause in the last years of his life? Why did he risk reputation, friendship, family and public approval to become the parliamentary spokesman of the despised and persecuted antislavery movement? Why did this most conservative statesman seek to upset the established order by abolishing the institution of slavery?

The answers to these questions can be found in the highlights of Adams's life.

First, the Adamses were conservatives by intellectual persuasion, not because of their wealth. Charles Francis was the first wealthy Adams, and this may explain some of his early opposition to his father's latter-day activities. Like his own father, John Quincy was a man of modest means whose material interests did not blind him to the higher interests of the nation. He broke with the Federalists when they advocated compromise to British sea power. The independence of the nation was more important to him than the profits of the New England merchants in the maritime trade. This position made Adams an outcast in the society of the Boston Brahmins, but it also prepared him for a conflict of far larger dimensions some thirty years later. By then the Federalists had been replaced by the Whigs, who chose to yield to the demands of the slaveholders in order to preserve the markets of Northern manufacturers in the South. Adams hoisted a banner of revolt. He believed the immorality of slavery was poisoning the spiritual wells of the nation and that the two systems of free-labor capitalism and chattel slavery could not exist indefinitely within the same Union. The Whigs retaliated in bitter enmity—but this time social ostracism held no terrors for Adams.

Second, Adams was ambitious, but there were certain boundaries he would not cross in pursuit of his career. Certain principles were sacred to him, and he held to them regardless of consequences. Had he been willing to play the British game, he might have been ambassador to the Court of St. James's before the age of thirty. Instead, he returned in a high dudgeon to his minor post in the Netherlands. Had he been willing to support the Federalist position, his own position in the Senate would have been assured. All he had to do was to hold his tongue. The Louisiana Purchase and the embargo acts would have passed without his vote. Instead he placed his head on the political chopping block because he had to do what was right. If he maintained this costly standard of Puritan virtue in the prime of his career, it was entirely logical for him to bring the same standards to bear on the far more important battles that faced him at an age when personal ambition was a thing of the past.

Third, Adams was a man in search of a cause. This too was a religious strain of his Puritan background. There is a revealing confession in his diary which he entered less than two years before his death. "My aspirations," he wrote, "to live in the memory of after-ages as a benefactor of my country and of mankind have not received the sanction of my Maker." These aspirations were not new. They went back to his diplomatic career and in some way inspired his work in the acquisition of Florida. As President, he had hoped to play the role of "benefactor" by promoting public works and the advancement of science. It was as a member of Congress, however, that he found the great cause he was seeking—the abolition of slavery. He thrust himself into the fray with matchless courage and devotion, and never looked back.

In characteristic self-denigration, Adams underrated his achievement. The truth is that by reconquering the right of petition and by breaking the slaveholders' monopoly in Congress he had brought the end of slavery nearer. "What is it that has taken his name from the list of everyday statesmen and made it a household word?" asked Wendell Phillips, the silver-tongued abolitionist orator. "It is the last ten years [twelve is more correct], the heroic years of his life—years during which he has linked his memory forever with freedom of speech, and with the right of the humblest human being to be heard by the government."

How shall we judge so full and paradoxical a life? Only in the light of the heroic years. Old men do not generally don uniforms and go off to the wars. Adams did because there was a place for him in the front lines, and he had the fighting spirit that many younger men lacked. Ex-Presidents do not as a rule join unpopular causes. Adams did, and in so doing he gave his cause an immense prestige that it could have acquired in no other way. Of all his peers, only John Quincy Adams could be that kind of an old man.

Was he a great President? No. He was a President who became a great man.